D0861910

CATCHING FUNDAMENTALS AND TECHNIQUES

Bob Bennett

COACHES CHOICE™

ISBN: 1-58518-152-8

Library of Congress Catalog Card Number: 99-69205

Cover Design: Chuck Peters

Production Manager: Michelle A. Summers

Coaches Choice Books is a division of: Coaches Choice
P.O. Box 1828
Monterey, CA 93942
Web Site: http://www.coacheschoiceweb.com

DEDICATION

The greatest influence in my catching career was my high school coach, Ollie Bidwell. His attention to detail and his discipline changed my life and many other young men whom he coached. He was the first to teach me that footwork and rhythm in throwing were basic fundamentals that could lead to consistency.

His persistence, commitment and attention to detail are to be applauded. He gave me the background to begin my coaching career. I dedicate this book to him.

ACKNOWLEDGMENTS

In order to develop coaching skills, the most important factors are the athletes. For almost five decades youngsters of all age groups have allowed me the privilege of developing my catching techniques. Through them I have developed what skills I have.

Developing a background is another essential factor. Coaching skills are learned and passed on to others. I had the good fortune to have a high school coach, Ollie Bidwell, who was willing to pass his knowledge along to me. In college, the legendary Pete Beiden provided a wealth of knowledge in catching and all areas of baseball.

In the process of gathering information, there were many outstanding coaches who graciously shared their knowledge with me. I thank them all. No one coach invented the game or the teaching techniques for any position. It is all shared information.

CONTENTS

Chapter

PREFACE

This book, written for catchers and their coaches, is based on my experience as a catcher, as well as my 40-plus years of coaching. It focuses on the fundamental techniques and strategy that a catcher must learn in order to play the most demanding position on the baseball diamond.

In my previous book on catching, I used all the available data and research material that I could find as a backdrop for a discussion of other coaches' and catchers' ideas and techniques. As I sought information on catchers and catching, however, I could not help but notice the dearth of in-depth books on the subject.

Perhaps the lack of books reflects the limited number of catchers; after all, on a baseball team, there are far fewer catchers than there are players at any other position. Still, the importance of the catcher to the overall performance of the team mandates that the position be looked at closely.

Ironically, baseball fans and observers seem to comprehend the importance of a good catcher only when a team is lacking one. It is almost as though they expect the catcher to perform the most mundane of chores, yet cannot appreciate the fact that a competent catcher had to endure long hours of repetitive practice in order to make difficult plays seem routine.

For the coach, it is typically difficult to teach catchers than it is to teach the other fielders. At least three primary reasons can account for such a situation: (1) a general lack of knowledge about the position; (2) the minimum amount of information available on catching; and (3) the difficulty in organizing practice to include drills that specifically help the catcher.

As a consequence, I wrote this in an attempt to shed some much-needed light on the topic for the coach and assist him and his catcher in a number of areas, including: the selection and use of the proper catching equipment; the techniques for selecting players for the catcher position; how to develop the fundamental catching skills; identifying and understanding proper practice habits; developing and employing drills to enhance essential skills; developing an appreciation of specific psychological factors and their implications for the catcher; and developing sound strategy.

This book is not about shortcuts. It is about coaches helping catchers develop the skills that promote consistency and accuracy. The fundamentals taught in this book require commitment and persistence. To the extent that this book enhances the ability of a catcher to play to the best of his God-given talent, then the time and energy involved in writing it will have been worth the effort.

Bob Bennett
Fresno State

CHAPTER 1

Tools Of The Trade:
Equipment Recommendations

By its very nature, the catcher position is the most dangerous of all. To be sure, no other player faces nine innings of bombardment by foul tips, bouncing pitches, thrown bats, and base runners barreling toward home plate. It is therefore imperative that the catcher wear the proper equipment that will provide him with the protection he needs. Despite the fact that young players are often indifferent to the care, inspection, and selection of their equipment, it is vital that each catcher have his own equipment and be responsible for it. Every piece of his equipment should be properly adjusted to fit his individual needs.

For maximum safety and performance, all catchers should wear the following: (1) a protective cup; (2) a snug-fitting chest protector; (3) shin guards that cover their kneecaps when crouching; (4) a mask that offers adequate protection to their face, ears, and neck; and (5) a mitt that enables them to become good receivers.

MASK

Catchers have a choice of two distinct types of masks—a wire mask and a bar mask. The wire mask has always provided the catcher with greater visibility than the bar-type mask, and it has been improved on in recent years. The bar mask, on the other hand, is light, but does not provide good visibility on low pitches.

The mask acts as a shock absorber. One that is too light or too small will not provide adequate shock absorption. Regardless of the debate over which mask is actually the best, however, the catcher should base his selection on personal preference. In observing professional and college players, it is obvious to me that both types of masks are used effectively. Perhaps the rule to follow, therefore, would be to select a mask that can best be used by that particular catcher, as he keeps in mind safety, comfort, and visibility.

After he puts on his mask, the catcher should adjust the straps so that the mask fits snugly. The rule of thumb is that the mask should be wide enough to cover his ears, and long enough to cover his throat. In the latter regard, the catcher needs either a flap or an extension on the mask to protect his throat as much as possible.

An ill-fitting mask is unsafe, and the catcher will need to test the fit by moving around quickly to see if the mask shifts. Since a loose-fitting mask will not offer him enough protection, the catcher will have to look for another one if the mask he initially selects does not fit.

CHEST PROTECTOR

When it comes to choosing a chest protector, the catcher must make sure not only that his chest protector fits properly, but that it also affords him the maximum protection—possibly at the cost of comfort. Many catchers do not properly adjust their chest protector. As such, many catchers tend to wear their chest protector too low, where it will not adequately protect their throat and collar bone. A catcher should also keep in mind that a chest protector should also fit snugly around the catcher's waist and chin and stay close to his body. A snug fit affords the catcher the ultimate in protection and also allows him a free range of motion, a factor which is an absolute necessity when one considers all the running and throwing that a catcher does is considered.

For added safety, many catchers now use a catching protector, an item that has an extra flap to cover the catcher's left shoulder. This flap is designed to minimize the possibility of injury to that part of the body. Roy Campanella, the former great Dodgers' catcher, introduced the chest protector with the extra flap back in the 1950s and used it with unqualified success. Some catchers now even use a protector with an extra flap that protects their throwing shoulder. Often, however, as with many innovations, certain aspects prove disadvantageous. Such is the case, for example, with the extra flap on the chest protector: Because it covers their entire shoulder area, many catchers complain that the flap hampers them when they catch the ball.

SHIN GUARDS

The shin guards should cover the knees when the catcher assumes the crouching position. Many shin guards appear long enough when standing, but are much too short when the catcher positions himself to receive a low pitch. The shin guards should also fit snugly and protect the kneecaps and insteps. The clasps on the shin guards should be worn on the outside.

When the shin guards are slightly short and offer only partial protection for the knees, the upper two elastic bands may be worn in a criss-cross fashion. This step forces the guards upward, thereby offering much needed protection for the knees.

PROTECTIVE CUP

Catchers are required to wear a protective cup during practice, as well as games. Although many young players find the cup uncomfortable and may even develop a rash from wearing it, it is the way the cup is worn that is usually the cause of the problem, rather than the piece of equipment itself. The catcher can solve the chafing problem by simply wearing two regular athletic supporters and placing the cup between the two of them. This step holds the cup higher and closer to the body and practically eliminates any rubbing in the groin area. All coaches should remember the cup is one piece of catcher's equipment that is not optional. For safety reasons, no player should be allowed behind the plate without a cup.

MITT

One of the first decisions a catcher or a coach must make about the position of catcher is the selection of a mitt. Although most coaches would probably prefer that the catcher choose a no-hinge mitt, chances are, the catcher will choose the more commonplace hinge mitt. The hinge mitt is big and flexible with a deep pocket that traps the baseball and allows for easy one-handed catches. It stands in stark contrast to the old-time leather pad that was practically flat, with a small pocket. While the no-hinge mitt, on the other hand, has a good-size pocket, it does not offer the flexibility of a hinge mitt, and requires two hands when catching the ball.

As a rule, a young catcher currently playing baseball will have trouble finding a no-hinge mitt, even if he wants one, because that type cannot be found on the shelves of most sporting goods stores. Instead, it must be ordered specially. What catchers will see when they go shopping is a variety of mitts with big webs and deep pockets. Although the hinge mitt is in great demand and is used almost exclusively, its advantages cut like a double-edged sword. On the one hand, the hinge mitt is a lot easier to use; on the other hand, it promotes lazy habits and poor footwork. Therefore, the key is for the catcher to use the hinge mitt to his advantage, while remembering to shift his body so that the ball stays in front of him.

Diagram 1-1: The Hinge Mitt　　　　　　**Diagram 1-2: The No-Hinge Mitt**

A warning about hinge mitts is in order: Because many of them are too flexible, they often cause injuries to the catching hand, particularly to the thumb. Therefore, care should be taken by the catcher to maintain solid work habits as he uses this particular mitt, so that he steers clear of injuries that can occur because of his laziness and sloppiness.

In the early days of baseball, catchers had no choice. The face of their mitt was virtually flat, and the pocket of the mitt was developed only through heavy use. The mitt had no web, and the space between the body of the mitt and the thumb was interlaced with strands of leather, making that space very narrow. A player using this mitt was required to get his body in front of the pitch and use both hands to make a catch. The mitt stopped the ball, and the catcher's bare hand closed in to either keep the ball in the mitt or take the ball out to throw it. In short, the old-time mitt forced the catcher to receive, rather than snare, the ball.

As the game evolved, the catcher's mitt was slowly upgraded. The space between the thumb and body was increased slightly, and a circular woven leather piece was inserted to hold the thumb and body of the mitt together in what is now referred to as a web. Although the web was not used as the normal catching spot, it did allow the catcher a little more catching surface for difficult-to-reach pitches.

The first really noticeable change in the catcher's mitt was the development of a break, or hinge, which made the mitt more flexible. Thanks to this innovation, the catcher could now squeeze the mitt around the ball for an easier, more secure catch. He could also catch the ball deftly with one hand. By the mid-1950s, the one-handed catch had become popular, and the mitts, even more flexible. Eventually, the catcher's mitt came to resemble a first baseman's glove.

The evolution of the catcher's mitt has affected the catcher position dramatically. While some would argue that the mitt has revolutionized the catcher position, others would complain that the changes have not come without a price. For example, since the catcher can make a one-handed catch with the hinge mitt, he is more likely to do so. At the same time, though, he becomes seduced into thinking that he need not shift his body in order to receive the ball. As a result, he often fails to keep the ball in front of him. The problem is compounded when the catcher tries to make a throw to a base, only to find that the ball is so deeply embedded in the pocket that he cannot accomplish the following tasks in time to nab the runner: (1) move his bare hand toward the mitt to retrieve the ball; (2) grip the ball properly, across the wide seams; (3) bring the ball into the throwing motion while he (4) shifts his weight so that he is in a position to push off for a hard throw; and (5) throw the ball with accuracy.

It is imperative that the catcher who relies on the ease and comfort of the hinge mitt also rely on his athletic ability and footwork drills. He cannot use the hinge mitt as a substitute for sound fundamentals. Rather, he should make the hinge mitt adapt to his existing mastery of sound techniques.

Clearly, the hinge mitt makes it easier for the catcher to do a number of things including, trap the ball and hold onto it; make the reception without having to get in front of the ball; make the tag at home plate; reach and catch a wide or high throw from the pitcher or another fielder; hold onto pop flies that force the catcher to reach over a fence; keep from dropping pitches; and handle short-hop throws in the dirt from infielders and outfielders.

The no-hinge mitt, almost a tool of the past, is no doubt bothersome to the average catcher. It not only cuts down his range on wide or high throws and makes for a difficult tag play at home plate, but it also forces him to shift his weight more often so that he can catch the ball with two hands.

Even the no-hinge mitt has its advantages, however. For example, a no-hinge mitt forces the catcher to develop the good habit of getting his body in front of the ball. It also encourages him to use both hands in catching and throwing. Furthermore, it promotes soft hands by causing the catcher to give with the catch. It also helps the catcher place himself in a more favorable throwing position. In addition, a no-hinge mitt helps him get the proper grip on the ball. It also helps him get in the right position for blocking low pitches. Finally, a no-hinge mitt promotes footwork and helps the catcher maintain his balance.

In the long run, it seems to matter little which mitt the catcher uses. What matters most are the catcher's work habits-the same habits he will take with him on the diamond. As for his mitt, if the catcher adheres to sound fundamentals, he will find the flexible mitt to be a tremendous advantage. If, however, he has become lazy and has developed the habit of using the hinge mitt in place of footwork, he is better off reverting to the no-hinge mitt and relearning the essential fundamentals.

HOW TO WEAR THE MITT

Each catcher should determine how he is going to wear his mitt. However, he should always take care not to push his fingers too deeply into the mitt or leave too much of the heel of his hand exposed. Neither of those two extreme actions will help his game. Instead, the catcher should insert his fingers all the way into the mitt so that they are deep enough to control the mitt as it properly bends from the fingertips to the heel of the mitt. (One of the problems with the hinge mitt, incidentally, is that the break is in the wrong place, a feature that makes the mitt bend with the thumb and little finger coming together.)

None of the catcher's fingers should be out of his mitt unless the mitt has an index finger protector on the back. The reason many catchers put their index finger on the back of the mitt is to gain more of a cushion. Yet the same kind of cushion can be provided by using a batting glove or a pad. Keeping the index finger outside of the mitt is a dangerous practice. At least four ways exist that the index finger can be injured by leaving the finger outside the mitt: (1) getting hit with a foul tip; (2) bending the finger back while diving for a foul ball; (3) getting the finger caught on the uniform of an opponent while making a tag play; and (4) getting the finger caught on the fence while attempting to catch a pop fly.

Because the mitt is obviously such a very important piece of equipment for the catcher, the mitt's lacing should be replaced periodically. The web should be checked frequently in order to prevent it from ever becoming loose. A loose web can cause serious injury to the thumb, as can a mitt that is too flexible.

Incidentally, one of the problems with the flexible hinge mitt is that the break is in the wrong place, making the mitt bend with the thumb and little finger coming together. Accordingly, a catcher using a flexible hinge mitt should relax his hand, but also stay completely in control of the mitt.

A good catcher learns to use his mitt properly. He learns to give with the pitch and cradle the ball, rather than grab it or snare it. He realizes that a good reception not only helps his own cause but that of the pitcher.

CONDITIONING AND CARE OF THE MITT

Although some guidelines exist that the catcher should keep in mind when choosing a mitt, he should look for a mitt that suits his individual needs. In time, with the help of his coach, the catcher will learn how to break in his mitt properly. By doing so, the catcher will learn to provide himself with a good catching area inside his mitt and learn how to shape it as though it has no web.

One excellent way to maintain a good pocket in the mitt is for the catcher to work the mitt by hitting the pocket side with the back part of his hand, in order to keep the mitt open. Another common practice used in shaping new mitts is to first place one or two baseballs in the pocket of the mitt. The mitt should then be formed around the baseballs. Finally, a piece of cloth or a belt should be placed around the mitt to hold it in the shape it is in and allow the mitt to hold that shape for at least one full day. Many catchers wet the leather before placing the baseballs in the pocket by wrapping it and placing it in a tub of water to soak. While this soaking method makes the leather easier to shape, it does take two to three weeks for the mitt to dry. This procedure also causes the leather to become dry and firm, therefore rendering the mitt virtually useless to a catcher who prefers using a loose mitt.

Catchers who prefer the firm, stiff mitt do not usually advocate the use of oil on the leather. If oil is used, it should only be placed on the areas of the mitt where cracking is prevalent. It should be remembered that failure to oil the glove most certainly reduces the glove's longevity. On the other hand, oily leather is soft and usually becomes shapeless. The shapeless, oily mitt may last longer, but there is some doubt about the kind of service the catcher can get from it.

Another popular practice for making the mitt more workable and more durable is to have the pocket, as well as the area near the web that receives the most punishment, reinforced with an extra strip of leather. Placing or sewing an extra leather strip onto these reinforced areas adds greatly to the strength of the mitt and also helps it to maintain its proper shape.

Above all, the catcher should be taught to take pride in his mitt, as well as in the rest of his equipment. When he packs his gear, the catcher should place his mitt on top of his other gear, or else he should carry it outside his bag. It takes a great deal of time and effort to work a mitt into shape, and that care should not be nullified by one carelessly planned road trip.

Most professional catchers are quite particular with their equipment. They feel that it is unwise to allow their mitt to be used by others. Each catcher has different-sized hands. Furthermore, each catches the ball in a different place in the mitt. As such, even a slight degree of variance in how the mitt is used can make a difference. Even more important, not all players who use a catcher's mitt will be conscientious about its care. A particular player may not be at all concerned about how the mitt should be used. Accordingly, for best results, a mitt should only be used by its owner.

HELMET

The catcher's helmet is as important to the catcher as the protective cup. Not only does the helmet offer added protection against low pitches that take bad hops, but it also protects the catcher from foul tips. In addition, the catcher's helmet helps prevent serious injuries when the batter completes his swing with one arm and strikes the catcher with his bat. A helmet also helps to protect the catcher on low pitches. The danger with low pitches is that they can bounce off the catcher's unprotected head as he tucks his chin into his chest before going down to block the ball.

EQUIPMENT BAG

Since each catcher is in charge of his own equipment, he should have an equipment bag which is used solely for his own catching equipment. The equipment can then be neatly packed, thus extending the life of his catcher's gear. The bag need not be large and bulky. lin fact, it should be just large enough for his catching equipment, thereby minimizing the chance of overpacking. As mentioned earlier, the catcher's mitt should always be placed on top of the bag so it cannot possibly be crushed.

CHAPTER 2

How to Select a Catcher

SIZE

As a rule, most positions in any sport lend themselves to athletes with certain body types. In football, for example, the fullback is expected to be big and powerful. In basketball, the center should be tall. Baseball, however, tends to be more of an equal opportunity sport. Although the first baseman often tends to be of above-average height, he does not have to be tall in order to play the position. The same holds true for the catcher, who need not be tall or short or for that matter big or small.

Personally, I prefer a tall, husky catcher, because his body type offers a good target and can absorb the pounding that goes with the job. Then again, other observers disagree, claiming that a short, stocky catcher is ideal.

A look at the history of baseball appears to substantiate the fact that catchers come in all shapes and sizes: Almost all body types are represented among a list of great catchers. Even a review of the literature, as well as interviews with professional players, scouts, and coaches, reveals that there are no specific size requirements for the catcher position. In fact, the possibilities are endless. What may be surprising to some is that the experts maintain that even a left-hander is acceptable as a catcher and should not be considered as a handicap in any way. In the end, it really matters little what a catcher looks like, for size and shape alone are not nearly as important as the catcher's level of stamina and agility.

STAMINA

One of the truly important attributes for the catching position is stamina. Almost without exception, most experts insist that the catcher, regardless of size, be durable and possess a great deal of stamina. Bending, squatting, and moving quickly after all kinds of pitches, along with backing up bases, blocking home plate, and doing lots of throwing, all tax the catcher's level of muscular endurance. The constant strain on his knees and the stress of calling pitches also help test his courage and toughness, as well as his stamina and endurance.

AGILITY

Although foot speed is a desirable trait in a catcher, it is not uppermost in the minds of most coaches, simply because most catchers are not fast runners. A catcher's agility level, however, is of paramount importance. For example if a catcher can quickly shift his body and get in front of the ball, or go down and block pitches, he can be a tremendous asset to his team.

LEADERSHIP

The catcher is often called the quarterback of the baseball team, and for good reason. Of all nine players on the diamond, the catcher is the athlete most visible to everyone else—the one who has the best view of the other fielders. The catcher is also the player the coach depends on to relay signals to his teammates and to call the pitches for his battery mate. All of these duties, in fact, make it incumbent on the catcher to display smart, aggressive leadership—the top priority for a catcher. It is through his leadership that a catcher can inspire his team.

The catcher is the only player positioned in front of all other team members. His attitude, therefore, is very important. The catcher should be a vibrant, energetic person. He should exude confidence and transfer that confidence to his pitcher and his teammates. Not surprisingly, the catcher is often called the quarterback of the baseball team.

Catchers are like any other leaders, however. Some are vocal, while others are more reserved and lead by example. Even though it is true that many great catchers were not great talkers, they had great confidence. Furthermore, they were able to relay that confidence to their teammates.

It is truly a rarity to find a successful team that does not also have a catcher who is a good leader. In reality, it is natural for the catcher to run the game. He is the general who plans, originates, and puts into operation the defensive plays of the baseball game.

HAND-EYE COORDINATION

A prerequisite for any good catcher is the ability to catch all types of thrown balls. Because of the variety of throws he sees and the plays in which he is involved, it is mandatory that the catcher have quick and agile hands. His ability to receive thrown balls smoothly and quickly is of the utmost importance. If he lacks good hand-eye coordination, the catcher will have a substantial amount of trouble with that aspect of his game.

A catcher who has difficulty in moving smoothly to receive pitches is a hindrance to the umpire as well as the pitcher. Not only does he make it difficult for the umpire to judge balls and strikes, he also forces the pitcher to modify his pitches in order to make it easier on the catcher. The results can be disastrous for the defensive team.

In addition to moving around smoothly, the catcher must be able to move quickly so he can handle a variety of throws and batted balls. The catcher must quickly catch and prepare to throw the ball. He must also be ready to handle pitches in the dirt, as well as bunts. A catcher with poor hand-eye coordination will find it nearly impossible to perform these chores adequately.

THROWING ABILITY

Although a strong throwing arm is an obvious asset for a catcher and a sure way to get the attention of the coach, many catchers have been successful despite not being blessed with a strong arm. Certainly, if a player is available who can throw hard and get rid of the ball quickly, he will have a better chance of becoming a success than will the catcher with a weak arm. Yet strength and quickness do not necessarily go together. Some players are slow in getting the ball away, but throw the ball hard; others are quick in releasing the ball, but do not throw hard. A player in either of these categories, however, can still be a good catcher. The strong-armed catcher who gets the ball away slowly can compensate for his weakness by simply throwing the ball with good speed. The player who lacks arm strength can make up for his lack of speed by getting rid of the ball quickly and then by throwing it accurately.

It is important to note that many players with strong throwing arms have difficulty with their control. At times, their throws are very difficult for their teammates to handle. If that is the case, the catcher will be forced to concentrate on maintaining his balance so he can throw accurately, which is exactly what the player with a weak arm must be able to do.

AGGRESSIVENESS

The catcher is the only player on the field who not only faces all the other players, but also has a hand in every single pitch of the ball game. Therefore, it is imperative that he be eager and enthusiastic, and that he channel those positive traits into an aggressive style of play. Whereas the slow, lazy catcher is a liability to his team, the energetic catcher is an invaluable asset. His positive actions can not only help the pitching staff, but also spur on the team as a whole.

INTELLIGENCE

The catcher must be smart and have good baseball knowledge. He must also be athletic and mentally alert. As far as actual intelligence is concerned, however, it is difficult to gauge the level a catcher needs. If it is true that most good catchers are leaders who work well with others, then it should follow that they also possess the ability to be sensitive to the personality traits of the pitcher they are catching. Accordingly, catchers, out of necessity, are probably at least of average intelligence, and, more than likely, above average.

Even though the catcher interacts with all the fielders, it is his relationship with the pitcher that is most intense and most vital to the team's success. The catcher must be able to assess a pitcher's reaction to criticism from the coach, as well as the pitcher's ability to handle stressful game situations and poor outings. Therefore, it is essential that the catcher should also be blessed with an above average level of common sense. The catcher who has common sense and a mind that is inquisitive enough to explore each challenging situation is way ahead of the game.

CHAPTER 3

Developing the Fundamental Skills

The importance of teaching a baseball player the fundamental skills of his position, and then encouraging him to master those skills, is unquestioned. During spring training, for example, major league coaches practice fundamentals by the hour. For their part, college and high school coaches generally spend a major portion of the entire season drilling on basic skills and maneuvers. What differs from coach to coach, however, is the approach to teaching these fundamentals. Thus it is important to keep in mind that even though the focus is always on teaching the fundamentals, the techniques employed to actually teach those fundamentals can vary quite a bit. Since this book focuses on the position of the catcher (a position that is generally agreed to be the most difficult position on the team to coach and master), the following sections were written to help both teacher and pupil master the process for learning the basic fundamentals attendant to being a catcher.

STANCE

In order to shift his weight quickly and efficiently, the catcher must assume the proper stance behind the plate. A good stance must afford him both comfort and mobility. Accordingly, the catcher should make sure his feet are spread about as wide apart as his shoulders, with his left foot slightly in front of his right foot. The catcher's weight, meanwhile, should be almost evenly distributed, with slightly more weight on his left foot, because his glove hand must travel farther when he shifts to his right. Since the catcher's ability to move quickly is of the utmost importance, his weight should be on the balls of his feet, not on his toes or heels.

It is also important that the catcher assume a low position. On the other hand, if his buttocks are too close to his heels, his weight will transfer to his heels and thus hamper his mobility. Accordingly, the catcher's ideal stance should be low, but not low enough to allow his rear to drag. Some catchers are able to keep their rear down and still move quickly, but most catchers cannot stay that low and maintain their mobility. Ideally, the catcher's rear should be as high as possible, without making him feel awkward. When the catcher is in his ready position, his rear should be at least even with his knees.

By staying low at all times, the catcher not only gives the pitcher a better target, but he also gives the umpire a better view of the pitch. Furthermore, by staying low, the catcher is better able to block low pitches and, at the same time, compensate for the fact that moving down to meet the ball takes longer than it does to move up to meet it.

Another important element of the catcher's stance are the positions of the catcher's hands and elbows, which should all be relaxed, but with the elbows held slightly outward. If the catcher keeps his elbows in, he may have trouble receiving low pitches. In the meantime, his mitt hand should be in a relaxed position and should not be overly extended toward the pitcher. His right thumb should be tucked under his index finger for added protection. If his hands are relaxed, as they should be, the catcher will be able to receive every type of pitch with more ease. Furthermore, if a foul tip should hit him on his relaxed hand, there will be less chance of serious injury than if his hand were tensed up.

Although the catcher should remember to remain comfortable by keeping his right hand at his side or behind his mitt, he must also be sure to move both his hands toward the pitch. Incidentally, the catcher's back muscles are more relaxed when either his bare hand or his mitt hand is down at his side.

It is important that the catcher take a position as close to the hitter as possible. He should not get so close that he will be hit by the bat or risk being called for catcher's interference. On the other hand, he should be close enough to offer the pitcher a good target, to be able to handle bad pitches, and to give the umpire a good view. The catcher should position himself so that by extending his glove hand, he can almost touch the batter's back elbow.

Diagram 3-1: The stance

Diagram 3-2: The stance

RECEIVING THE BALL

A good catcher makes catching look easy. Thanks to his soft, relaxed hands, a pitch or throw that hits his glove appears to suddenly, yet quietly, stop. A good catcher also receives the ball with one hand, while he keeps his bare hand close by to either help with the catch or grab the ball and prepare it for throwing. To help him develop soft hands, the catcher should keep his hands and wrists flexible.

The catcher must learn to shift his body weight so that he can get in front of the ball. At the same time, he must let the ball come to him. Reaching or grabbing for the ball will create tension in his hands and arms.

In order to make effective catches, the catcher must learn to relax, because relaxed hands are able to move quickly and accurately. He should wait for the ball. The catcher who waits for the ball will be able to concentrate harder on the ball. That focus will make it easier for him to catch foul tips and low pitches. Keep in mind, of course, that the catcher should still be aggressive when he moves to catch wide pitches. In those instances, he should move quickly to get in the area of the pitch and then allow his hands to relax as the ball reaches his mitt.

After the pitcher releases the ball, the catcher should prepare himself for the pitch. In order to best prepare, he should relax his hands by turning his palms slightly upward, with his fingers bent, so he will be able to move his hands quickly. Since any early movement he makes could disturb the pitcher's concentration, the catcher should not move until the pitcher has released the ball. The catcher should position his hands like an infielder who is preparing to move toward a ground ball.

A good catcher must learn to cushion the ball by pulling back slightly as the ball makes contact with his mitt. With good timing and relaxation, the catcher should be able to make receiving and cushioning look relatively easy.

It is the catcher's duty to do his best on every pitch thrown. Therefore, he should find a stance that enables him to shift for any thrown ball. Even without men on base, it is a good idea for the catcher to try to stop every pitch, regardless of where it is thrown. By being aggressive in this regard, the catcher will better earn the pitcher's trust and confidence, as well as that of his teammates.

Because footwork and rhythm are both important when it comes to receiving the ball, the catcher must work on both aspects in order to master them. Once the catcher's movements feel natural, he will be much more able to move around smoothly and to give the umpire a better view of the pitch.

Not only does a clean catch make the catcher look sharp, but it also helps the pitcher. It is, after all, on those borderline pitches that a "smooth" catcher can increase the chances of a called strike. To help get the call on a close, inside pitch, for instance, the catcher should turn the palm side of his mitt toward the outside portion of the plate and then smoothly bring it up into the strike zone. On outside pitches, the reverse holds true. On low pitches, the palm side of the catcher's mitt should be turned upward, while on high pitches, the palm should face downward. If the catcher follows these guidelines, he can help the pitcher on many close pitches.

It should be noted that the catcher is not cheating when he catches the ball into the strike zone. Instead, what he is doing is merely working to make sure that a strike will look like a strike to the umpire. The catcher should never try to pull bad pitches into the strike zone. The umpire will usually know what the catcher is up to and perhaps be tempted to take even the borderline strike away from the pitcher.

FRAMING THE PITCH

Accordingly, what is referred to as "framing" pitches should not be construed as the catcher taking liberties on a pitch, but rather simply bringing the ball toward the center of his body and, hence, toward the strike zone. To frame a pitch merely means to keep the ball in the frame of the strike zone with soft hands. While a fringe pitch, for example, will look better to the umpire if the catcher receives it smoothly, it may look like a ball to the umpire if the catcher makes jerky movements on it.

Diagram 3-3: Framing

Diagram 3-4: Framing

Diagram 3-5: Framing

Diagram 3-6: Framing

Soft hands are important to a catcher when he frames a pitch. As for his arms, they should be outstretched and bent slightly at the elbows. His mitt and bare hand, meantime, should be close together and relaxed. As he gives the pitcher a target, the catcher should keep his thumbs together, relaxed and ready, and rotate them up and to the sides. By using this technique, the catcher will be placing his hands in a position to catch either a low or a high pitch. Once the pitcher releases the ball, the catcher should rotate his mitt and bare hand approximately one quarter of a turn from the target position.

RECEIVING THE LOW PITCH

The catcher who can block or catch pitches in the dirt is, of course, a great asset to both his pitcher and his team. The catcher who cannot is a liability, because the pitcher may find it necessary to overcompensate for the catcher's suspect blocking abilities by throwing his pitches—especially his curveball—higher than he should-an act that can result in serious trouble.

If the catcher is aggressive and mobile, he should be able to stop low pitches. However, he should go about the task realistically. His aim should be to block the ball, not to catch it. Attempting to catch every low pitch tends to lead to excessive movement with the mitt, an action that can cause many low pitches to get by the catcher. Instead, the catcher should try to move his body in front of the ball and make sure his mitt always moves under the ball. He should then either block the ball or knock it down. Most importantly, the catcher should attempt to keep the ball in front of him.

Of course, it would be helpful if the catcher would anticipate that every pitch is going to be a bad pitch. By anticipating a wild pitch, the catcher is keeping himself alert and ready for it. For example, if he expects a curve, the catcher should be ready to receive the ball regardless of where it is thrown. Since the curveball rotates downward and breaks away from the hitter, the catcher should anticipate moving in that direction. While anticipating a wild curveball, the catcher should put slightly more weight on his left foot in order to ready himself to move low and to his right.

In blocking the low pitch, the catcher must put his body in the path of the ball. In order to do that effectively, he must keep his shoulders parallel to the pitching rubber and his chin tucked in. These movements will form angles that will help the catcher keep the ball in front of his body. If his shoulders are not parallel to the pitching rubber, the angle at which the ball hits his body will cause the ball to be deflected to his side and behind him. The catcher should make every effort to keep the ball out in front of him. In this regard, he can help himself immensely by keeping his mitt and his bare hand low and in front of his body, relaxing his hands, and thinking of blocking the ball instead of catching it.

Passed balls are usually a result of poor (i.e., lack of) anticipation. To prepare himself, the catcher should not allow himself to be fooled by a pitch. He should call the pitch and know how his pitcher is going to throw it, so that the pitch he receives never surprises him.

The catcher should study each pitcher in order to grasp the pitcher's tendencies. It can be quite helpful to the catcher to store information on each pitcher, making notes on the speed and break of each pitch. Armed with this knowledge, the catcher will be better able to anticipate what each pitch will do. If the pitcher tends to throw breaking pitches in the dirt, for example, the catcher should prepare to block those pitches.

Many pitchers are not as consistent as they should be. On one hand, they may throw several mediocre pitches, and then suddenly throw an outstanding pitch, such as a fastball, with exceptional movement or a curveball with a devastating break. These exceptions should be noted by the catcher, who should mentally prepare to catch those rarely thrown pitches. It will be easier, however, for the catcher to adjust to the mediocre pitches than to the rare good one. In realty, preparing for the tougher pitch will make the less well thrown pitch easier to catch.

Opinions vary on the proper way to block low pitches. Some catching coaches advocate forming a cup with the body to block pitches. Others promote a tall, soft method. Both methods are effective. As always, success depends on the work ethic, commitment, and ability of the catcher.

The cup method requires the catcher to drop to both knees and get himself in front of the pitch. He blocks the ball by forming a curve with his upper body that traps the baseball. Proponents of this style of blocking low pitches teach the catcher to stay low, get in front of the ball with both knees, and hover over the ball. The cup formed by the upper body should therefore keep the ball from getting by the catcher. With the cup method, the catcher holds his mitt low to the ground and keeps his knees pointed outward. The mitt thus blocks the area between his legs. On viewing the low pitch, the catcher must move quickly in the diirection of the pitch and get both his knees on the ground to block it.

The tall, soft method of blocking low pitches, on the other hand, enables the catcher to move more quickly, and is really more functional than the cup method. The rules for performing this method are simple. The catcher drops to the knee nearest the ball. If the ball is directly in front of the catcher, though, he should drop to both knees. In either case, the catcher will find that the softest way to get down is to lower his buttocks before he drops to his knees.

After he drops down, the catcher should keep his shoulders parallel to the pitching rubber. He should make himself as tall as possible and try to make his body soft. He should also try to create angles with his body so he can keep the ball out in front of him. He accomplishes this by tucking his chin in and turning his shoulders. His mitt, meanwhile, should be on the ground and held out in front of him (even with his chin), with the mitt's pocket facing the ball. It is vital that the catcher not allow the pocket to face upward. When using the tall, soft method, the catcher should be very active with his mitt by keeping it low and moving it from side to side. He should be less active, however, with his up-and-down movement, because such action may allow the ball to get under his mitt.

If the ball is to the catcher's right, he should lower his buttocks and drop to his right knee; he should also turn his right shoulder toward the pitching rubber and keep his chin tucked in. The catcher should also bend his right foot and keep his front cleats in contact with the ground. He should let his right knee gain ground to get around the ball, a maneuver that will place his right leg at approximately a 45-degree angle. By following these rules, the catcher will be in a better push-off position to recover and retrieve the blocked ball or to recover and make a throw. If the ball is to the catcher's left, he should lower his buttocks and drop to his left knee and use the same fundamentals as he would with his right knee.

Diagram 3-7: Low pitches to the catcher's right

Diagram 3-8: Low pitchers to the catcher's left

Diagram 3-9: Low pitch, directly in front of the catcher

GENERAL SUGGESTIONS FOR A CATCHER ON LOW PITCHES

- Stay low.

- Be relaxed.

- Keep your eyes on the ball.

- Keep your body in a direct line with the ball.

- Be ready to move quickly.

- Block the ball and keep it in front of you.

THROWING GRIP

The throwing grip determines how the catcher will release the ball and the degree of spin he will put on it. If he grips the ball too loosely, it will not have enough spin. If he grips it too tightly, the muscles in his hand, wrist, and arm will tighten and have an adverse effect on the spin of the ball, because the tightness will interfere with the snapping of his wrist. The ball will spin more quickly if the catcher's grip is just firm enough to allow his other muscles to relax so that he can get achieve the maximum snap of the wrist.

To ensure a good grip, the catcher should follow a check system in which the coach examines the firmness of the catcher's grip. First, the coach should warn the catcher that he will be asked to stop during his throwing procedure. Next, the coach should have the catcher grip the ball, start his throw, and then stop, making sure that the catcher holds the ball in such a way that the ball can be removed from his hand, but, at the same time, maintain some level of resistance on the ball. . The coach should then remove the ball from the catcher's grasp and examine the catcher's grip to determine how firm it is.

A well-balanced grip consists of holding the ball with the pads of the fingertips gripping across the seams at the widest spread of the seams. The index and middle fingers should be spread slightly, and the thumb should be tucked underneath. The thumb should bisect the index and middle fingers; the third and fourth fingers should not touch the ball during the throw. If there is interference from the third and fourth fingers, the ball will probably not travel as far as it should, and it may fade to the right side of the infield.

The catcher and his coach should pay special attention to the meaning of "across-the-seam grip" (i.e., the ball is gripped with the fingertip pads across the wide seams and not the narrow seams). Gripping the ball across the seams at the point where the seams are the narrowest makes the ball rotate the same as it would when gripping the ball with the fingers along the seams. Gripping the ball with the seams causes the ball to sail or to sink.

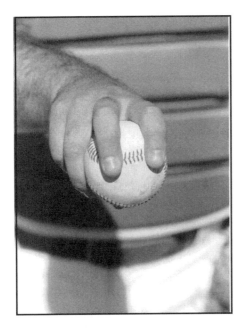

Diagram 3-10

Diagram 3-11

In preparing to throw the ball, the catcher should find the proper grip as he brings the ball up into throwing position. By concentrating on this aspect every time he makes a catch, the catcher will be able to learn to grip the ball across the seams automatically. It will take commitment and practice on the catcher's part to perfect his grip and to make such a grip a habit.

Another indispensable habit that will help the catcher get a good grip on the ball is using both hands to catch the ball. As soon as the ball hits his mitt, the catcher should move his bare hand in and grip the ball. Regardless of how he initially grips the ball, however, the catcher will need no more than a quarter of a turn to secure the desired grip, and to make any necessary adjustment on the ball as he brings the ball into the ready position for a throw. The catcher should use his mitt and his bare hand together in order to adjust his grip, a maneuver that can be done smoothly and that can become part of his throwing rhythm. As a matter of fact, the time it takes the catcher to get the proper grip will have a major impact on his throwing rhythm. The catcher's grip is very important because it is the major factor in causing the ball to spin, and spinning affects the speed of the ball as well as its direction and flight pattern. Many things affect the thrown ball, including gravity, wind resistance, velocity, and, of course, grip.

In the case of the catcher's throw, if it is directly overhand, the ball should spin backwards off his fingers to create increased air pressure at the bottom of the ball and reduced pressure at the top of the ball. This I action will keep the ball in the air longer and will cause the ball to be better able to overcome the effects of gravity. If the catcher grips the ball improperly and causes it to spin forward like a curveball, the reduced pressure will be at the bottom of the ball. As a consequence, the increased pressure will be at the top of the ball, causing it to move downward or to curve.

THROWING

Throwing involves many principles of movement. One of the primary principles is velocity. By the time the ball leaves the hand, the body has completed its supply of power to the ball. Force is supplied by muscle strength. Muscle strength starts momentum, and the momentum is transferred from the body to the thrown object. The methods used for developing speed and controlling the direction of the hand, therefore, are of prime importance. Before developing these methods however, it would be beneficial to review the mechanics of throwing.

First, the arm forms an arc and rotates around the shoulder axis. If the arc is long, then more time exists to build power and also more leverage exists. Hand acceleration is important, too. The longer the backswing of the hand, the more time there is to build up momentum. Rotation of the hips toward the backswing helps to build this momentum. In reality, all factors considered, the more parts of the body that are involved in throwing the ball, the faster the ball will be thrown. It should be kept in mind, however, that when many parts of the body are involved, sequence and timing also become important factors in throwing the baseball.

Another factor that determines the velocity of a throw is the movement of all the contributing parts of the body in the direction of the throw. All factors considered, if all the actions are directed toward the target, the ball will be thrown faster. Again, however, timing is involved because of the transfer of the pitcher's weight. The method in which the weight is transferred is critical, because if the weight is transferred against a stiff leg, resistance is present and momentum is slowed, resulting in less speed. If the weight is transferred onto a bent-front leg, the regular sequence of movement is enhanced. The result will be more speed on the throw.

Running or hopping into the throw will increase its velocity, because the momentum of the body enhances the arm swing. For example, outfielders and infielders use a hop or sometimes a running step when time is not a factor. Time, however, is always a factor for the catcher.

The release point is another major factor in determining the speed of a throw. When the release coincides with the instant of maximum momentum of the hand, the ball will travel with greater speed. The maximum momentum of the hand is reached at the center of the arc of the throw. For the catcher making an overhand throw, this point will be about even with the bill of his cap. Any act, such as jerking or stopping, that creates a different release point reduces the speed of the throw.

Many of the factors that affect the speed of the thrown ball are likely to decrease the catcher's control of the direction of the throw. For example, the longer the arc, the more difficult the control of direction. In building speed, it is important to employ as many body segments as possible. On the other hand, if control of the ball is the main objective, the use of fewer body segments would be a wiser approach.

The catcher's throw actually starts with the catch. The catcher should shift for the ball first, then shift back so his weight is on his right foot. His wrist should be bent forward, his grip should be firm, and his arm should be relaxed. His wrist and elbow should be held high, with his elbow about as high as his shoulder. Meanwhile, his throwing hand should be clear of his head, and his elbow joint should be bent at about a 90-degree angle. Contrary to what many observers believe, the catcher does not cock the ball behind the ear. In fact, he should not cock the ball at all. Rather, his throw should be rhythmical and continuous if it is to be quick and accurate. His arm should be extended as the ball is released, and the snap of the catcher's wrist should come at the last moment. After releasing the ball, his arm should be in line with the target. It should be noted that the catcher's arm should not come down in the same manner as the pitcher's arm.

Most of the throws made by the catcher should be directly overhand. A sidearm or underarm throw causes the ball to rotate improperly. Although certain plays may make it necessary to throw from a position other than overhand, this deviation should be the exception rather than the rule.

When the catcher throws the ball, he should not pause during the throwing motion. He should simply catch the ball and bring it directly into the throwing position. While the ball is on its way to the throwing position, the catcher should secure the proper grip, which will make it possible to continue with the throw without any hesitation.

The catcher should establish a rhythm when he throws the ball. In this regard, as an aid, he may find it helpful to use a counting system. The complete action of catching and throwing should be done in three counts. The coach or catcher may refer to the counts as "catch, one, throw," or as "one, two, three." In the beginning, as he is establishing his rhythm by way of the counting system, the catcher should use a slow count. He should still make sure that every move is done at the same speed. The three steps, or counts, are as follows: (1) Emphasis should be placed on securing the proper grip. The speed at which he acquires the proper grip will determine the pace of his rhythm. Time the catch so that the forward step and the catch occur simultaneously; (2) get the proper grip while bringing the ball into the throwing

Diagram 3-12: Throwing—almost a 90-degree angle: the elbow should be held as high as the shoulder

Diagram 3-13: Follow through position—extend the arm toward the target, snap the wrist at the last moment.

position; and (3) throw the ball in rhythm. The catcher will be able to learn to grip the ball across the seams automatically. With practice, the catcher can consistently grip the ball across the seams. He must make this a habit by acquiring this grip each time he plays catch. It is possible to locate the proper grip on each throw.

Using both hands to catch a ball helps the catcher get the proper grip. As soon as the ball hits the mitt, the catcher's bare hand should move in and grip the ball. Regardless of how the ball is initially gripped, it will take no more than a quarter of a turn to secure the desired grip. This adjustment can be made as the ball is being brought into a ready position to throw. It is necessary to use the mitt and the bare hand together to adjust the grip. This can be done smoothly and become part of the throwing rhythm. As a matter of fact, the time it takes to get the grip determines the throwing rhythm.

The speed at which the catcher moves will depend entirely upon his own ability and level of experience. The only way for him to develop rhythm is to practice the count every time a catch and throw occurs. Once he develops his rhythm, he will find that he no longer needs to count. If this rhythm becomes irregular after a time, however, the catcher should go back to the counting system. What the counting system really does is to provide the catcher with a base of operation. He can always return to it if he encounters difficulties in throwing.

FOOTWORK

Catchers at all levels use many different footwork systems. Yet, even though all major league catchers, for instance, do not use the same type of footwork, each employs some type of footwork, nonetheless. Clearly, opinions about the use of footwork vary, for even the experts do not all agree on any one particular procedure. Most experts agree, however, that shifting for pitches is advantageous and, in some cases, absolutely necessary.

Coaches and catchers should keep in mind that as valuable as footwork is, it can be overdone. For example, if the catcher moves too far and jumps around while receiving pitches he is apt to make the umpire's job difficult. He might also tend to overshift and thereby upset his balance, making it difficult to throw.

Proper shifting is important for two reasons: it makes catching the ball easier because it helps the catcher center his body in front of the ball; and it makes throwing the ball much easier because of the better balance it provides. In shifting, the basic idea is for the catcher to step into the path of the ball. If the ball is thrown to his left, he should step to his left with his left foot. If the ball is thrown to his right, he should step to his right with his right foot. If the catcher follows this technique, his body will always be moving to the ball.

A variety of terms are used by experts to emphasize shifting to get in front of the ball. A term that makes sense is to "funnel the ball." Accordingly, the catcher should thus think of his arms and hands as a funnel, drawing all throws toward the center of his body. Another approach is to encourage the catcher to catch every ball in line with his nose, a move that will force him to shift his weight to get into a good fielding position.

After receiving the ball, the catcher should clear himself from the hitter by stepping away and toward the base to which the throw is to be made. In the process, he should always use his right foot as a pivot point, or a base from which to push off with his right foot. A good push-off is helpful to the catcher because it adds speed to his throw. Consequently, he should place his push-off foot at about a 45-degree angle, a move that adheres to the same principle applied by pitchers when they push off the pitching rubber with their pivot foot. By placing his foot down at this angle, the catcher allows his hips and shoulders to rotate, thereby creating greater acceleration.

The catcher should never let himself get caught in a position that will necessitate throwing through or over a hitter. Such a situation not only can lead to errors, but is also apt to result in injury to the catcher or the hitter. While some catchers may try to throw over or around the hitter, no real advantage exists to doing that. A better approach is for the catcher to clear himself from the batter and get his throw off easier and faster simply by using the proper footwork.

The catcher can shift toward the ball and catch it in one count. On another count, he can bring the ball into the throwing position and clear from the hitter. By diligently working on these two counts, the catcher can place himself in a good position to make a throw on the count of three, and he can accomplish these steps without having to throw over the hitter.

FOOTWORK USED FOR THROWS TO SECOND BASE— RIGHT-HANDED HITTER

Outside pitch

- Step to the ball.

- Grip the ball and bring it up into the throwing position, since clearing-the basic requirement for planting his foot in the No. 2 position-is already completed.

- Throw the ball.

Diagram 3-14: Footwork for the outside pitch with a right-handed batter.

FOOTWORK USED FOR THROWING TO SECOND BASE—RIGHT-HANDED BATTER

Inside pitch

- Step to the pitch.

- Clear himself from the batter, stepping to the No. 2 position; Get the ball into the throwing position.

- Throw the ball.

Diagram 3-15: Footwork for the inside pitch with a right-handed batter.

FOOTWORK USED FOR THROWS TO SECOND BASE—LEFT-HANDED BATTER

OUTSIDE PITCH

- Step to the pitch.
- On this particular pitch, the catcher is actually clearing from the batter as he steps to the pitch. He should then plant his right foot in the No. 2 position. While stepping to the No. 2 position, he should be getting the ball into the throwing position.
- Throw the ball.

Diagram 3-16: Footwork for outside pitch with a left-handed batter.

Diagram 3-17: Footwork for inside pitch with a left-handed batter.

FOOTWORK USED FOR THROWS TO THIRD BASE

Diagram 3-18 Footwork for inside pitch to right-handed batter on throws to third base.

Diagram 3-19: Footwork for inside pitch to right-handed batter on throws to third base.

- Step to the pitch.
- The catcher must clear himself by moving his right foot behind his left, as shown in Diagram 3-18, so that he can move behind the batter and toward third base.
- Throw the ball.

NOTE: With a left-handed batter, the catcher will have no problems with clearance. The same footwork can be used, but the catcher will not have to worry about throwing behind or in front of the batter.

In order to learn the fundamentals of footwork, the catcher must be committed. Often, he must learn to break old habits, which is often more difficult than starting fresh and learning a new skills. If the catcher has the desire to learn the proper footwork, then he must be active and tuned in. It is important, therefore, that despite the hazards and rigors of catching, he does not give in to laziness or weariness or sloppiness.

A catcher who uses the proper footwork puts himself in a good position to catch and throw. He is balanced. He is in control of his body. His footwork creates consistency. The development of consistent footwork, however, requires regular practice. This practice must carry over to game situations. The catcher must learn to move to each pitch until that movement becomes second nature to him. He should then follow up what he has drilled on in practice by using those techniques during each ball game.

It is important that the catcher realize that footwork is not something he can do only once in a while. Accordingly, it should be his ultimate goal to maintain the habit of moving to the ball, with the intention of timing his catch with his step. Both the catcher and his coach, however, must be truly dedicated if they intend to achieve the goal of imbuing the catcher with this valuable habit. Toward that end, a few minutes of daily drills can pay great dividends. In learning how to catch the ball, clear from the hitter, and throw in rhythm, it is important that the catcher pay attention to details and be diligent in forming the basic skills of the proper techniques. Once the catcher learns the proper footwork, he should nonetheless continue with daily footwork drills.

FIELDING BUNTS

If the catcher is to accurately and consistently field bunts, he must use both his mitt and his bare hand. Scooping the ball with both hands not only adds to the effectiveness of fielding the ball, but allows the catcher to begin locating the proper grip on the ball sooner, resulting in better control of his throws. Although on rare occasions the catcher may find it necessary to bare-hand the ball and make a quick throw, picking the ball up with the bare hand is a very poor habit. It should definitely be the exception rather than the rule.

When he fields a bunt, the catcher should keep his body in line with the base to which he is throwing. At times, he will find that he has to circle or half-circle the ball in order to maintain that position. As an aid, in this regard, the catcher should keep his body low, with his knees bent, as he fields the ball.

The catcher is responsible for a 13-foot semicircle in front of home plate. If the ball goes beyond this semicircle, the catcher's chances of making a successful play will be limited, and one of his teammates should be in a better position to make the play. Any ball within this semicircle, however, should be fielded by the catcher, and he should be able to make the play himself. On occasion, the catcher may be called upon to cover a greater area. However, but still, his chances of success will be lessened. Even though the prescribed area is considered to be his territory, he should commit to field all bunted balls, no matter what area they are in.

It is also imperative on the bunt play that the catcher be alert and get a good jump. He must get rid of his mask quickly and toss it out of the way without wasting time. Many professional catchers assume a slightly higher stance when anticipating a bunt. However, some experts advocate that a regular stance be used when catching a pitcher who has poor control. Accordingly, the regular stance is recommended for high school and college catchers, since they are more likely to be catching those kinds of pitchers. The higher stance offers an advantage to the big-league catcher: and it allows the catcher to get a faster start. By raising the rear about two to three inches and moving forward as the ball is bunted, the catcher is able to get to the bunted ball quickly.

FIELDING BUNTS

General Suggestions:

- Watch situations—be ready to move.

- Observe the batter. He will sometimes give the bunt away by his movements or by his position in the box.

- Be aggressive.

- Scoop and throw the ball in one continuous motion.

Diagram 3-20: Fielding position for bunts—the catcher should get in position so that he is in line with the throwing target.

If the catcher cannot field the bunt, he must call out the base to which the ball should be thrown. On a bunted ball fielded by the third baseman with a runner on first base, the catcher should call the play and then cover third base. In the larger sense, the catcher is responsible for alerting the other players to possible bunt situations. In doing so, he must discipline himself to assess all possible plays that may arise.

On all bunted balls, the catcher should also be anticipating a double play, and should always make that his top priority when assessing the particular player should assess the play from that standpoint. He should start by picturing a double play in his mind. Then, as the play unfolds, he should be aware of factors that may cause him to change his mind and call for the ball to be thrown to first base instead (e.g., a runner who got an exceptional jump; the type of bunt or its speed; the speed and position of the fielders; etc.). Because the aggressive catcher anticipates a double play, he is more likely to be able to make any necessary adjustments. The passive catcher, on the other hand, anticipates getting one out. As such, he is usually reluctant to try to throw out the lead runner.

CALLING PLAYS

During each at-bat, the catcher should be thinking in advance about the game situation and should remind the other fielders—especially the third baseman, the first baseman, and the pitcher—about the plays they will possibly have to make. The catcher should respond quickly, decisively, and loudly to each situation and use verbal commands and hand-and-arm signals. When the ball is hit, It is always a good idea for the catcher to step in front of home plate and point to the appropriate base at the same time he is calling the play so he will be able to minimize confusion.

Certainly, one of the most important roles the catcher plays is that of decision maker. As such, he must learn to accept this role without fear. One thing is clear: it is better that the catcher make the wrong decision than to be indecisive or make no decision at all. If he is paying attention, as he should, the catcher will always be aware of conditions that might help his decision making: the inning, the number of outs, the score, the speed of the base runner, the position or jump that the runner gets on the play, the speed of the fielders, the strength of the fielders' arms, and the condition of the field.

The catcher should think aggressively. On bunted balls, for example, he should work from the premise that he will be throwing to nail the lead runner. From that point, he should continue his decision-making process with "possibility thinking". As the play unfolds, the catcher should look at the picture that is being painted. If something appears that warrants a change from his original plan, he should take that into account before making a final judgment.

The catcher should carefully observe the details and nuances of each situation. One of those details, for example, may lead to his calling for the throw to be made to first base. The lead runner may have left too early; the pitcher or infielder may have broken in too slowly; the ball may have been bunted too weakly. Any number of factors may be enough cause for the play to be made at first base. The point for catcher's to internalize is to start with aggressive, rather than conservative, intentions. Catchers learn by making mistakes. Consequently, all factors considered, an aggressive mistake is much better than a timid mistake.

Another key factor in assuming the role of decision maker is the inflection of the catcher's voice when he calls plays. His voice should be short, sharp, demanding, and loud. He should develop a distinctive sound that is easily recognized by his teammates. The catcher who develops self-confidence will present a more positive picture to his teammates and will also be more likely to intimidate the opposing players.

PICKOFF PLAYS

On pickoff attempts, the catcher should simply use the same throwing technique he uses with normal throws, making sure he catches the ball and clears himself from the batter before throwing the ball. It is important, however, that despite being set up to make a good throw, the catcher should not throw just for the sake of throwing. Instead, he should wait until the runners are too far off the base. Often this play will be spontaneous. At other times, however, it may be necessary to set up the runner for the pickoff. The best way to set him up is to make him believe that he is being ignored by letting him inch away to a good lead as the ball is thrown back to the pitcher.

Another way to set up the runner is to have the pitcher lob the ball to first, almost methodically, thus encouraging the runner to take liberties. Once the runner is lulled into a false sense of security, the time is ripe for the pitcher to fire the ball to first quickly in an honest-to-goodness attempt to pick him off.

As profitable as it is to pick runners off, however, the catcher should be cautioned against overusing the pickoff play. Overuse of this play can destroy the element of surprise-a factor that is vital to the success of this play. The catcher should also figure that he has a very good chance of picking off the runner, or else he should not bother to make the throw. Because each time the catcher throws the ball, he is risking an error, the attempted pickoff should be worth that risk.

Prudence, however, should not make the catcher tentative about attempting a pickoff. An aggressive catcher who makes good, quick throws behind runners helps to set up double plays. His pickoff attempts also keep runners honest and thus help to prevent them from taking an extra base on singles. As such, it is easy to see how a smart, alert catcher can help keep his pitcher out of jams.

For the sake of his pitcher and fellow infielders—as well as the outfielders who may be called on to back up an overthrow—the catcher needs to work out a set of signals for the pickoff and a signal for the pitchout. The catcher's indication that a play will include a pitchout and a pickoff, however, should be given as one signal so that the fielders will be ready to break when the pitcher throws the ball outside the strike zone. If the catcher signals for a pickoff only, the infielders will have to wait until the ball is swung at or taken by the hitter before they can reveal their intentions and race to the bag for the throw.

The pitchout can present a problem for the catcher, who often finds himself unable to maintain his balance because he has made the mistake of stepping with his right foot first. Instead, if he brings his left foot over, next to his right foot, and then steps out to the pitch with his right foot, he will be better able to make a quick throw from this balanced position. If he steps with his right foot first, the catcher will be handicapped by an unusually wide stride position that makes it hard for him to keep his balance. On the other hand, if he steps with his left foot and then his right foot, he will allow himself to shift his weight evenly and smoothly. (If the batter is left-handed, the catcher should simply move his right foot even with his left foot and then step out for the pitchout with his left foot.)

A bunting situation offers an excellent opportunity for a pickoff play or a pitchout, because runners often get anxious and leave their base before the ball is bunted. In fact, any situation that creates anxiety in the runner gives the catcher with a good chance to pick him off base. Anxiety is often increased when the batter swings at the ball, because the runner anticipates that the ball will be hit; therefore, when the ball is swung at and missed, the catcher may have an opportunity to catch the runner off base with a quick throw.

When the bases are loaded, the catcher has an excellent opportunity to pick off runners at first or second base because these runners are often ignored. As such, they frequently take careless leads off the bag. If he is willing to take advantage of these opportunities, the catcher has an excellent chance of helping his team through many difficult situations.

As for the other infielders, they should not wait for the catcher to signal a pitchout or pickoff. Instead, they should be ready at all times to take a quick throw from the catcher, who may not have time to call the play, but is reacting to a particular situation. The key to initiating a pickoff is alertness. As such, the catcher who keeps his head in the game often finds opportune moments to trap a runner off base.

The catcher, like the pitcher, should have different kinds of pickoff moves. A catcher who has a variety of pickoff moves will be better able to keep the runner closer to the bag than he wants to be. The catcher's standard pickoff move to first base, regardless of whether the batter is right-handed or left-handed, entails rotating his body toward first base, shifting his weight to his right foot, and making a regular overhand throw to the first baseman. In this situation, the only adjustment that the catcher will have to make from time to time is that he will have to throw *behind* the left-handed batter.

Another pickoff method calls for the catcher to stay in his stance and throw to first base by rotating his upper body. On this play, the catcher does not move his feet. He simply shifts his weight to the inside part of his right foot to start the throw, and then shifts his weight to the inside part of his left foot when he makes the throw. This movement is similar to the shoulder pivot of a second baseman making a feed to the shortstop; his power is generated by the weight shift and his upper body.

A third pickoff move that can be used by the catcher is another one that does not involve the catcher moving his feet. In this move, he drops to his left knee as he rotates his shoulder to make the throw to first base, much like the second baseman who feeds the shortstop. This move also lends itself to a side-arm delivery, a movement that is best used by more experienced catchers. Because the overhand throw remains the more consistent of the two, it is recommended for younger catchers.

Another excellent pickoff move—one that requires good balance and flexibility— calls for the catcher to step toward the pitcher before turning his shoulders to make a throw to first base. The first part of the throw should appear to the runner to be a throw back to the pitcher. In this scenario, the catcher should look directly at the pitcher as he strides on his left foot. Next, the catcher should raise his arm into the throwing position. As his stride foot contacts the ground, the catcher should rotate his shoulders and make a quick throw to first base. He should not look at first base until he turns his shoulders. Some catchers continue to look at the pitcher during the throw. Although this look is more deceptive, it is less consistent. It really is not necessary for the catcher to keep his eyes on the pitcher during the entire process, because the deception is created by the position of the catcher's body during his stride. By keeping his shoulders parallel to the pitching rubber and his eyes directed at the pitcher during the stride, the catcher will appear to be throwing to the pitcher. If this move is carried out properly, the catcher will be able to look at first base as his shoulders make the quick change of direction for the throw to first base.

TAGGING RUNNERS AT HOME PLATE

Many plays at home plate do not require the catcher to block the plate. In fact, there are times when blocking the plate is unwise. When the catcher has plenty of time to tag a runner who makes no attempt to slide, or if the catcher is slightly in front of the plate and moves out to meet the runner, no need exists for the catcher to block or make heavy contact with the runner. In these instances, the catcher should place the ball in his mitt and maintain the proper throwing grip while tagging the runner. He should make the tag and give with the runner's force. It is unwise to emulate a football player on this play. As the runner is tagged, the catcher should step to one side and tag the runner with very little contact, thus minimizing the chance of having the ball knocked loose and freeing the catcher up to make any play that may be subsequently be needed.

On the other hand, some times exist when the catcher will be required to block the plate. A good technique to use in blocking the plate is for the catcher to place his left heel at the edge of the inside corner of the plate, with his toe pointing toward third base. This stance permits the runner to slide for the back point or outside half of the plate. If he places his right foot directly behind his left foot and keeps his feet spread in a position that provides balance, the catcher will be able to brace himself for the hard-sliding runner. If the runner slides to the outside half of the plate, the catcher should drop to his left knee and hip in front of the runner to make the tag. The runner's power will be somewhat diminished by the hook or fadeaway slide. Therefore, the necessity for the catcher to brace himself is not as great.

A runner often attempts to run over the catcher in an effort to knock the ball out of his hands. Provided adequate time is available, a method exists that can protect and help the catcher in tagging this kind of runner. In this scenario, the catcher should attempt to stay very low and then come up quickly at about the moment the runner makes contact. This move will cause the runner to absorb most of the shock of the impact and allow him to be more easily controlled and tagged.

Many plays call for the catcher to move out to get the ball and then dive back onto home plate. On this type of play, the catcher must avoid diving past the plate, because such an action could be very hazardous. It is essential that the catcher holds the ball with both his mitt and his throwing hand. After making the tag, the catcher should quickly ready himself for the next play. While diving onto the plate is very dangerous and should not be common practice, it is sometimes necessary when the throw loses force or is off target.

Throws from outfielders are often difficult for the catcher to field because they usually hit the grass in front of him and take unpredictable bounces. The catcher is often caught flat-footed or moving away from the throw because he placed himself in a set position when the throw approached. To be safe, the catcher should position himself approximately two steps behind the plate and then move into the throw as it bounces. This action enables him to move toward the ball and to get in the tag position at the same time. Starting behind the plate affords the catcher more time to look at the ball which, in turn, allows him to judge the bounce of the ball and move accordingly.

Taking a position approximately two steps behind the plate gives the catcher a good view of the entire play, from where he can assess the position of the fielder and see the position of the baserunner. If the catcher is receiving a throw from the outfielder, he is able to determine the throwing distance and whether the runner has a chance to score.

When the outfielder comes in contact with the ball, the catcher should make his first decision. If the outfielder is within his throwing range, the catcher anticipates letting the ball come through. As the outfielder picks up the ball, the catcher looks at the position of the baserunner. If the base runner has not reached third base yet, is at third base, or is no more than two steps past the base, the catcher anticipates letting the throw come through.

Next, the catcher should read the throw. If the throw is weak, the catcher should have the ball cut off by the cutoff man. If the throw is off line, the catcher should have the ball cut off. Other factors to be considered are the situation and the jump and speed of the runner.

On throws from the outfield, the catcher normally discards his mask. However, wearing the mask on these throws would actually be to his benefit. The mask can offer protection on collisions with a baserunner. It also protects the catcher's face from a bad-hop throw from the outfield. Consequently, with his mask on, the catcher is more apt to hang in on the play at the plate and the bad-hop throw.

Some coaches argue that the mask blocks the catcher's vision. In reality, however, that argument is not valid. During the course of a normal game, the catcher must catch many different kinds of pitches while wearing his mask. Certainly, a ball thrown from the outfield can be seen as easily as any of these pitches. It should be noted that the catcher who may be in the habit of discarding his mask when he does not need to, will have to practice this new habit of leaving his mask on in this situation.

FORCE PLAYS AT HOME PLATE

On force plays at home, the catcher should place one foot on home plate and open his body to, or face, the player who is throwing the ball. He must catch the ball while touching the base, clear himself from the batter/runner, and throw to first base. For example, if the ball comes from the third baseman, the catcher should place his left foot on the front part of home plate and his right foot to the right side of the infield. From this position he can catch the ball, thus forcing the runner at ome, and then pivot, with his weight shifting to his right foot, and throw the ball (inside the first-base line) to first in an attempt to complete the double play.

On throws coming from the first baseman, the catcher should place his right foot on home plate and his left foot on the third-base side of the infield. Before throwing back to the first baseman, the catcher must clear himself from the batter/runner by bringing his right foot behind his left foot and toward the infield.

When the batter/runner is certain to reach first base safely, it is sometimes wise to make a full arm fake after pivoting and then throw to third base with the possibility of getting a runner who might be taking a wide turn at third.

On throws that are off line and difficult to catch, the catcher should forget about completing a second throw for a double play. Instead, he should concentrate solely on making the catch and getting the force at home plate. After getting the out, he should clear himself from the area. When the bases are loaded, the catcher should step out in front of the plate and remind the pitcher, the first baseman, and the third baseman of the possible play at home plate.

POP FLIES

On a pop fly, the catcher should take his mask off quickly and hold it until he determines the direction of the ball. Once he does, he should toss the mask a good distance in the opposite direction. The mask should not be discarded carelessly, however, because hasty mask throwing can result in injury or error or both.

Several factors impinge on the fielding of pop flies, including the type of ball park where the game is being played. If it is an enclosed ball park, the ball will have greater movement when it gets up higher than the top of the stands, because the wind will no longer be blocked out. Because there is nothing to stop the ball from suddenly reacting to the wind, the ball will often shift unpredictably. Wind has a great deal to do with the action of a pop fly. Strong winds cause the ball to move violently. Strong winds also affect the ball's rotation, thereby making the pop fly more difficult to catch.

The sun can also affect the catcher who is trying to catch a pop fly. Therefore, it is smart to always give priority on the play to the fielder with his back to the sun, assuming he and the catcher have an equal chance of catching the pop-up.

On a pop fly, the ball normally rotates toward the infield. The force of its rotation, however, will depend on how the ball comes off the bat, how hard it is hit, how high it is hit, the type of stadium in which it is hit, and the strength of the wind. These factors should all be considered in fielding pop-ups and should routinely be checked before every game. As such, the catcher can help himself tremendously through his pre-game observations.

The catcher may field pop flies by either facing the infield, turning his back to the infield, or turning sideways to the infield. If the catcher fields the ball while facing the infield, he should get under the pop-up so that it is in line with his forehead as the ball starts its downward flight. The ball's natural rotation will carry it to a position approximately two feet in front of the catcher's forehead.

If the catcher chooses to field the ball with his back to the infield, he should position himself to allow for the ball's rotation. Since the pop fly normally rotates toward the infield, the catcher, when he faces the backstop, should be careful not to overrun the ball. On the ball's downward flight, the catcher should judge the rotation of the ball and allow for approximately two feet of rotation. If the catcher is facing the backstop, the ball will rotate toward him. When fielding pop flies with his side to the infield, the catcher should also consider the natural rotation of the ball toward the infield and allow for this movement.

The catcher is responsible for aiding the third baseman and the first baseman when either is fielding a pop-up. In both instances, he should move over so that he is in direct line with the ball. This action enables the infielder to use the catcher as a guide to indicate whether the ball is in the open or whether it is close to the fence or the dugout. If the ball *is* near the fence or the dugout, the catcher should move over and place one hand on the structure. This maneuver helps the fielder to judge the relationship of the ball to the catcher. Since the catcher is touching an obstacle, the fielder can see that the ball is also near the obstacle. The catcher should not only offer visual help, but should offer verbal assistance as well. He should tell the fielder whether there is adequate space to field the ball. It is also important that both the first and the third baseman reciprocate when the catcher fields the ball.

Communication on pop flies is essential. If two or more players are involved on any play, communication is an absolute necessity. One player must field the ball, and the other player, or players, must assist in the catch by giving way to the player making the catch. It is essential that all players involved in the play are sensitive to the need to avoid obstructing the player catching the ball. It is imperative that the player making the call be assured that he will be allowed to make the catch without interference from any of the other players. They should warn him by yelling, "Take it!" or "Lots of room!" or "Watch it, watch it!" or "No play!"

A warning to a player about an obstruction is as important as calling for the ball, because both calls can prevent injuries. A warning to a teammate who is near an obstacle can help to prevent injuries and can help to develop credibility and confidence among his teammates.

Diagram 3-21: Position of hands when catching pop flies—palms up.

Diagram 3-22: Position of hands when catching pop flies—thumbs together.

SIGNALS

In giving signals, the catcher should take his stance, remembering to keep his buttocks low. He should point his left knee at the short stop and his right knee at the second baseman, but he should not spread his knees too wide. His left arm, meantime, should rest on his left thigh. As a security measure, the catcher should allow his mitt to hang in front of his left knee. By doing so, the catcher will be able to prevent the third-base coach from seeing his signs. The catcher should also place his right hand directly in front of the cup area. It is immaterial whether he uses finger or hand signals. By following these procedures, the catcher will be also be able to shield his signals from the first-base coach. As a precaution, the catcher should use at least two sets of signals, because the runner on second base will often attempt to steal the signals and relay them to the batter. If the catcher thinks the runner is sneaking a look at his signals, he can switch to a second set of signals.

The signal system should be established before the game. In fact, all signals should be settled well before the game. A signal conference between the pitcher and the catcher at the start the game is a poor practice that frequently indicates that very little thought has gone into this particular aspect of the game.

Although it is important that signals be hidden from the opposing team, it is just as important that the signals be easily seen by the pitcher, shortstop, and second baseman. On the other hand, the signals should be simple because, all factors considered, it is better to have the other team see a signal than to have a teammate miss one.

When he calls the pitches, the catcher should use his background information on the hitter. If the catcher has been doing his homework, he should have a good idea about the hitter's strengths and weaknesses. If the catcher has never seen the hitter before, he might get some indication of the hitter's strengths and weaknesses by the type of stance the hitter uses, the position of his hands, the way he swings the bat in warm-ups, the manner in which he strides to hit, or any other information the catcher has picked up from scouting reports. All of these suggestions should be weighed by the catcher.

It should be noted that although scouting information is extremely valuable, it should be used sensibly. In other words, the catcher should consider the strengths and weaknesses of each opposing batter in relation to the strengths and weaknesses of his pitcher. Usually, the pitcher's control and overall ability are more significant than any information the catcher can find on the hitter.

SIGNALS

- Hand directly over crotch area.
- Left knee pointing at shortstop.
- Right knee pointing at second baseman.
- Mitt hanging in front of left knee
- Buttocks low.

Diagram 3-23: Stance for giving signals.

Signal Systems

For consistency, function, and simplicity, the catcher should number the various pitches and not allow those numbers to be changed. For example, the fastball is number one, the curveball is number two, the change-up is number three, and the slider is number four. By adhering to this rule, the catcher will be ensuring an easy transition to any other system.

In choosing a signal system, the catcher can use any of four basic systems: the flap system, the finger system, the pump system, or the mitt system.

Flap System

In the flap system, the catcher uses his bare hand as a flap and holds it in his cup area. When giving these signals, the catcher should use only his hand, and he should try to keep his arm in the same position for all signals. To signal for a fastball, he holds his flat hand against his cup. To call for a curveball, the catcher holds his hand in the same area and lifts his fingers so that the palm of his hand is parallel to the ground. To order a change-up, he wiggles his fingers. To call for a slider, he lifts one finger. Of course, if the pitcher throws more than the traditional four pitches, it will be necessary to expand the number of indicators used in the system.

Finger System

In this system, the catcher keeps his bare hand inside his right leg, near his groin area. He calls for the various pitches by holding out one or ore fingers in the following manner: fastball, one finger; curveball, two fingers; change-up, three fingers; slider, four fingers.

Pump System

The pump system (a system that has several versions) is widely used. One version calls for the catcher to signal a number first and then pump with his fingers. Thus, if he keeps the pitches and numbers in sequence, the catcher will be easily understood by the pitcher. The pump system is relatively straightforward. For example, the catcher holds out three fingers, a move which represents the starting point for the signals. The number three, meanwhile, is the first number in the count. Regardless of the number of fingers the catcher holds out, the pitcher simply counts the pumps. If the number three, for instance, is followed by three pumps, the catcher is calling for a curveball. In other words, the starting point was three, meaning that the catcher is calling for a change. The point is to stay in the sequence and count. If the catcher starts with the change-up and continue in sequence, the first pump after three will indicate a slider, the second pump will indicate a fastball, and the third and final pump will indicate a curveball. The point to remember is that three is a change-up (which is also the starting point). Abiding by the rule to stay in sequence, the pitcher has to count the pumps after the starting number; three, four, one, *two* are the numbers presented. Accordingly, two is the signal for a curveball. Another example might involve the catcher holding out one finger and following with two pumps, thus signaling for a change-up. One finger held out indicates that the counting sequence starts with one. Staying in sequence and counting, then, the numbers would be one (the starting point), two (for one pump), and three (for the second and final pump). Thus, three is the number that indicates a change-up. The number of fingers held out matters only with the first signal given. The number of fingers held out for each pump does not matter. The number of pumps is the key.

Mitt System

The mitt can be used for yet another set of signals. If the signals are given with the catcher's mitt, the other signals can be used as decoys. In this method, during the process of giving signals, the mitt is held in front of the catcher's left knee. With slight adjustments in that position, a set of signals can be developed. Holding the mitt directly in front of the knee, with the top of the thumb pointing at the pitcher is a signal for a fast ball. The curve ball signal can be given by holding the mitt on the outside of the left knee. Holding the mitt on the inside part of the knee requests a change up.

The signal for the slider is given by sliding the mitt over the front of the knee from left to right. When the mitt signals are in use, one or more of the other sets may be given but should be ignored by the pitcher and the defense.

Each signal system should be familiar to the pitching staff, the catchers, and the other defensive players so that the transition from one set to another will not result in confusion. In order to help avoid confusion, each set should be used often. During intrasquad games, in fact, it is a good idea to alternate systems so that the team will be able to switch its signs in pressure situations without disrupting anyone's concentration. If the opposing players are stealing the signs, a switch in systems should thwart them.

WHO SHOULD CALL THE PITCHES

Signal calling was once solely the catcher's responsibility, but no longer is this the case. Nowadays, the head coach or the pitching coach often handles the signal calling—much to the irritation of many a catcher.

The main reason some coaches decide to call the signals themselves is job security. These individuals believe that since their jobs are on the line, the important function of signal calling should not be left in someone else's hands. However, many other coaches disagree. They maintain that the game is taken away from the catcher when the coach calls the signals. Neither side is right or wrong, however, because both arguments involve good points.

Personally, I prefer that the catcher call the signals. First, he is closest to the hitter and is more likely to pick up important clues about the batter's style and intentions. Second, as the ball game and the season wear on, the catcher learns to develop a feel for the game. His awareness of each situation, combined with his ability to see and sense the hitter, gives the catcher an edge. When the coach calls the signals, that edge is ultimately wasted. Third, the catcher has the inside scoop on his pitcher and knows him better than anyone else. He has a partnership with the pitcher because the two have worked closely on a daily basis. Consequently, the catcher is the one player who is going to know which pitch is most likely to work for a particular pitcher at a particular point in time.

Furthermore, making the catcher responsible for calling the signals creates pride and leadership in that position because the catcher is visible to the entire team, his actions are mirrored to others. If he is forceful and aggressive, those traits will be transferred to his teammates. Thus, the more pride he takes in himself and in his position, the more valuable he will be to the team. Taking the signals out of the catcher's hands will take away some of his ability to direct the team. It is important to keep in mind that part of the job of a coach is to teach his players how to lead. It is simply a given that when the coach lets his players lead, when he lets them make decisions, they will make mistakes. Making his players accountable and responsible for those mistakes is an invaluable part of their learning process.

BACKING UP AND COVERING BASES

When first base is occupied, the catcher is responsible for covering third base if the third baseman fields a bunted or topped ball. Therefore, it is important that the catcher think of this possibility every time a runner is on first base. When the third baseman comes in to field the ball, the catcher shouts a loud verbal command and points to where the ball should be thrown. After making this call, the catcher should run over and cover third base.

With no one on base, the catcher should back up first base on all infield outs. He does this by moving up the first-base line, staying in foul territory a good distance from the bag, and aligning himself with the infielder who is throwing to the first baseman. The catcher, who will find it difficult to get in the line of throws from the third baseman and the shortstop, should move as far and as fast as possible. If he hustles, he may be able to retrieve some balls that get by the first baseman.

With the bases empty, the catcher should also back up first base on base hits and fly outs. This positioning will help on throws from the relay man or the outfielder who is trying to nail a runner who has rounded the base too far. If the batter hits a fly ball with a runner on first base, the catcher should also back up in case there is an attempt to throw behind the runner who has tagged up. In these instances, the catcher may actually be of assistance only once out of 50 times, but that one time may be the key play in the game.

When runners are trapped between third base and home plate, the catcher is responsible for chasing the trapped player back to third base. On this play, the catcher needs a fast start, he can get one by preparing to receive the ball from the third baseman and then moving to it so that the moment he catches the ball, he is also taking a running step. An attempt should be made to cut the number of throws to one—the throw from the catcher to the third baseman. It is generally not a good idea to allow the baserunner the opportunity to run back toward home plate. Instead, the trapped runner should always be forced away from home plate so that if an error is made or if the runner is safe, there is no advancement—the runner merely returns to his starting point.

SPECIAL PLAYS

In certain instances, the catcher is required to cover third base. For example, he should cover third base on bunted balls with a runner on first base, and also on any slow-hit balls that pull the third baseman into the infield and away from third base. The reason is that the third baseman may not be able to get back to the base in time for the play if the runner on first tries to advance to third.

The first-and-third situation is one of the most difficult scenarios for the catcher, because the catcher must catch the ball, look the runner back to third base, and then throw the runner out at second. On this play, however, the catcher has four alternatives. One option is the head fake. On this play, the catcher intends to throw the runner out at second base, but must check the runner at third before throwing to second. The look at the runner should cause him to go back toward third base, or it will provide the catcher with a good idea of the runner's distance from the base. If the runner at third base has too much of a lead, the catcher may decide to try to throw him out.

The second alternative is to use a full arm fake to second base to lure the runner off third base, and then throw to third base. After catching the ball, and prior to using the arm fake, the catcher should look the runner back to third base. He should then fake a throw to second, but make sure that his throwing motion is very deliberate. A common mistake by many catchers is to hurry the arm fake by using a short arc with their throwing arm so they can fire to third more quickly. What they should do, however, is to make their fake throw to second seem indistinguishable from their normal throwing action. The catcher, therefore, should take the time to move his arm the same way he does on a normal throw and to leave his arm at full extension for a moment. He should then step with his right to a point even with his extended throwing hand, thus placing himself in a position to throw to third base.

The third option is to look the runner back to third and then throw high to the pitcher, making his throw look like a throw through to second. The pitcher then catches the throw and fires to third to try to get the runner there. Again, this play should begin in the same way as the throw to second base. There must be a prearranged signal with the pitcher for this play.

The pitcher can help by staying in his follow-through position as long as possible, which will help make the throw appear to be going through to second base.

The fourth alternative is for the catcher to throw directly to either the second baseman or the shortstop. (The catcher will designate beforehand who will take the throw, but normally, the infielder covering the bag will take the throw from the catcher.) The infielder who is to receive the ball runs straight toward the catcher if the runner at first base attempts to steal. His job is to cut the throw off and then throw out the runner attempting to steal home. On this play, there is no attempt to throw out the runner going to second base. This option is a special play designed to keep the runner at third base from scoring, and it is a good play to use in key situations. The team using it is gambling that the runner will try to score. If the runner at third does not attempt to score, however, the gamble will not pay off. As a result, two runners will now be in scoring position.

Whichever first-and-third play the catcher decides to use will depend on the score, the inning, the number of outs, the speed of both runners, and the ability of the catcher and infielders. It is considered poor technique to hold the ball and make no throw at all, because the runner at first will, in effect, be given a free ticket to second base.

CATCHER'S DUTIES AFTER THE BATTER STRIKES OUT

After a strikeout with the bases empty, many catcher throw to third base to start the relay around the horn. However, a more practical habit is to throw to first base instead. If the umpire calls the catcher for trapping the third strike, the catcher will already have thrown to first base, thus enabling the first baseman to step on the bag for the out. On the other hand, the old routine of going to third base after the strikeout makes a more natural throw for the third baseman to throw the ball around the infield. As a safety precaution for the catcher, the throw to first base makes much more sense.

CHAPTER 4

Drills and Practice Techniques

One of the major reasons that the catcher position is probably the most difficult to coach is that much of the catcher's practice time—sometimes as much as half—involves warming up the pitchers. As a result, the catcher often cannot find enough time to practice on his own fundamentals. To help out, a team should have three or four catchers, who can rotate during pitcher warm-ups. Of course, the down side to this solution is that it is very difficult to give playing time to four catchers. If all four are alternated during practice, then none will have enough game experience to realize his full potential at the position.

Another reason coaches have trouble overseeing the progress of their catchers is that the coach is usually involved with the daily routine of hitting ground balls to infielders and fly balls to outfielders, to say nothing of the time he must spend giving instructions to the pitchers and the hitters. In reality, the coach typically finds it difficult to spend a great deal of time with the catcher. Furthermore, while many practice drills exist that involve the catcher, most of these drills are not specific to the catcher position.

As much, at the beginning of each season, a great deal of time should be spent with the catcher. Most teams require the pitchers and catchers to report for practice about two weeks before the other players. This early start provides an opportunity for the coach to help his catchers with their fundamentals, while the pitchers work on their conditioning program. By focusing more closely on his catcher, the coach will be providing him with a strong base of knowledge and a sense of responsibility—attributes that will eventually enable the catcher to work on many of the fundamentals by himself. If the fundamentals are emphasized and clearly presented to the catcher, he will be able to practice them during the warm-up period with the pitcher. He can also improve on his fundamentals during batting practice, infield practice, and even while playing catch.

Another potential problem area for catchers involves batting practice. Because of his many duties, the catcher is often shortchanged in batting practice. This situation, however, can be avoided by scheduling the catcher to take batting practice before he warms up his pitcher. He should be permitted to move ahead of every other player in the batting cage, and his teammates should be told ahead of time so that any hard feelings can be avoided.

The beginning of each practice is an excellent time to work with the catcher. While other players are involved with pepper games, warm-up drills, or batting practice, the coach can buy some time and help the catcher work on his fundamentals. For example, each practice could begin with a short session on fielding bunts, catching pop flies, practicing footwork, gripping the ball, throwing, blocking low pitches, or, for that matter, any of the skills involved in the catcher position. Spending 10 minutes a day on even one of these skills could help the catcher tremendously.

Many coaches encounter problems in finding drills for the catcher position because fewer published drills seem to exist for the catcher position than for any of the other positions. It is much easier, for example, to find instructive materials on pitching, hitting, or fielding drills than on catching.

The regular variety of activities in the daily workout can provide the catcher with work on many of his fundamentals. Simply taking the catcher through a regular daily workout without giving him individual help on his position, however, is not enough. Just like any other player, the catcher needs individual drills and individual help with his skills and techniques.

While literature dealing with the catching position is limited, it is possible to identify drills for this position. Experienced high school coaches, college coaches, and experts in the professional ranks are all excellent resource people for such unique drills. In addition, a coach or catcher may wish to create his own drills to meet his individual interests of requirements. After all, a drill is nothing more than repeated practice on a certain skill. To create a drill, it is necessary to break down the various skills required of the catcher. Therefore, if a coach or catcher develops an activity that causes the catcher to repeatedly perform one or more of these skills correctly, then a useful drill has been created.

DEVELOPING THE STANCE

A good stance is basic to good catching, but it is often difficult to learn. Many poor habits are developed by some catchers. In turn, these poor habits usually lead to problems with other catching skills. Such poor habits are often the result of laziness on the part of the catcher. In many instances, though, both the coach and the catcher are guilty of overlooking certain fundamentals. Therefore, as with all the other skills he will need, the catcher's ability to develop a good stance will depend on to a great extent on receiving sufficient guidance from his coach.

One method for checking and commenting on the catcher's stance is for the coach to place all his catchers in a line in front of him. Each catcher should assume his proper catching position, relaxed, with his weight evenly distributed on the balls of his feet. His body should be low and ready to move to either side. The coach then points in the direction to he wants the catcher to move. The catcher shifts to that position, then shifts back to his original position, enabling the coach to ascertain whether the catcher's weight is being properly distributed. If the catcher's weight is poorly distributed, then the catcher will have trouble shifting in either direction. The coach should then correct the catcher until the catcher is able to move to either side with agility and relative ease.

The scope of this drill can be broadened by using a ball. The coach gives directions by pointing with the ball, while the catchers assume their stance and move in the direction of the ball. The coach simulates a throw and holds the ball out in front to indicate a low-and-outside pitch. Each catcher should then shift to his right and simulate the catch. The coach, meanwhile, should note whether the catcher is shifting his weight properly. The coach continues with this procedure, requiring the catcher to shift and simulate catching pitches in all areas. Weight shift, mitt position, and footwork can all be highlighted.

FOOTWORK DRILL

The purpose of this drill is to help the catcher improve his ability to shift for all types of pitches. The catcher may practice shifting to the ball by taking throws from the coach, who throws the ball to the right, to the left, or straight at the catcher. It is best, at least in the beginning stages, that the coach tell the catcher the direction of the impending throw so that the catcher will be better able to concentrate on the proper footwork and weight distribution. His footwork will be determined by the location of the ball and by whether the batter is left-handed or right-handed. Each catcher should be given throws to his right, to his left, and straight to him, while both right-handed and left-handed batters take their normal stance. The catcher should practice stepping to the pitch, clearing himself from the hitter, and throwing the ball. It is suggested that the catcher run through the steps of this drill somewhat methodically at the outset, but as his ability to perform the drill improves, he works on conducting the drill at "game speed".

As the catcher becomes more familiar with his footwork, he should be able to adjust it to suit each pitch. Each catcher will project his stage of development by his reactions. He should learn, however, as quickly as possible to be able to automatically shift properly on each pitch. Once he does, he will be ready to catch in game situations.

It is also important that the catcher pay careful attention to coordinating the timing of each catch with his footwork so that he will be able to establish his rhythm. When the catcher steps to catch the ball, he must simultaneously ensure that the ball makes contact with his mitt. If he performs this maneuver properly, he will be in a better position to follow through with his throwing motion. The proper way for him to step and catch is to shift his weight to the ball of his foot as he steps to the ball. By transferring his weight in this manner, the catcher will be placing his weight over his foot. As a result, he will be better able to keep his balance. It is important to remember that proper balance is essential for the catcher to be able to make consistent throws.

FOOTWORK FOR THROWING TO THIRD BASE DRILL

The purpose of this drill is to help the catcher develop the proper technique for throwing to third base without hitting or throwing over a right-handed batter. In conducting the drill, the catcher should be told where the ball will be thrown so that he may concentrate specifically on his footwork. Pitches should be thrown to his left, to his right, and straight over the plate. The catcher should step to the pitch and throw either in front of the batter or behind the batter, depending on the location of the pitch. If the pitch is inside, the catcher should step to the pitch, then step behind the batter, and throw to third. He should begin this maneuver by stepping to the ball with his left foot. After making the catch, he should then take a drop step behind his left foot and throw to third base. At the same time that he takes the drop step, he should try to move closer to third base.

On a throw to the outside, the catcher should step toward the pitch and throw in front of the hitter. As he steps to the pitch with his right foot, he should drag his left leg toward the ball. This action will prevent his feet from spreading too wide apart. Often, catchers stride toward the outside pitch while their left foot remains stationary. In the process, the catchers lose their balance.

If the pitch comes directly over the plate, it is acceptable for the catcher to throw either in front of or behind the batter. However, the catcher should decide which is best for him and use the same procedure on all pitches down the middle. Each catcher will have a personal preference. Some will throw better by going behind the hitter, while others will throw better by going in front of the hitter. The important factor is consistency.

The same footwork is used when the batter is left-handed. In this case, however, the catcher does not have to worry about clearing himself from the hitter. As always, he should adhere to sound fundamentals.

To help beginning catchers, the coach should announce the direction the pitch will take, and he should then throw the ball gently, even tossing it. As the new player's skill improves, the coach should increase the speed of his throws and let the catcher guess which direction the throw will take by not announcing it as before. Once the catcher's footwork becomes automatic and smooth, he is ready for greater challenges.

DEVELOPING PROPER GRIP AND ROTATION ON THE BALL DRILL

This drill is excellent for the beginning catcher. All factors considered, it is also of great value to the experienced player as well, because it offers both athletes an opportunity to concentrate on gripping the ball properly without having to become involved with several other catching skills. Even seasoned players often encounter difficulties in gripping the ball-a problem that usually leads to poor rotation on the ball and, consequently, inaccurate throws. Because so many factors exist that can lead to gripping the ball improperly, this drill is extremely valuable to the catcher.

To conduct this drill, the catchers should be divided into groups of two players. Each catcher should assume a standing position, with his feet approximately as wide as his shoulders, and face his partner, who is about 50 to 60 feet away. (This distance can be lengthened to 90 feet, once the catcher has learned to maintain his balance at the shorter distance.) The primary objectives of this drill are for the catcher to concentrate on catching the ball; to secure his grip on the ball as he brings it up into the throwing motion; to enable the catcher to feel comfortable with the proper throwing position; and to allow him to throw with the proper ball rotation. This drill is not as effective if the catcher is forced to step to the pitch. As such, eliminating the footwork in this drill affords him the opportunity to concentrate solely on his grip.

For optimum results, the coach should carefully observe each catcher in order to see that he is using the proper mechanics. The catcher should begin gripping the ball immediately upon contact with his mitt, and he should continue turning the ball with his fingers until he finds the proper grip. He should locate the proper grip by the time he brings the ball into the throwing position, and there no hesitation should occur once the ball reaches the throwing position. No matter how he originally grabbed the ball after the catch it will take no more than one quarter of a turn of the ball to secure the proper grip. As he brings the ball up into the throwing position, the catcher should rotate his trunk slightly, while keeping his weight on the balls of his feet. He should then remember not to take any steps as he throws the ball. His throw should be made by extending his arm and rotating his trunk toward the throw, all the while continuing to maintain his balance.

The ball should spin backward off the index and middle fingers and should maintain this type of rotation throughout its flight. If the ball does not rotate properly, either the catcher's throwing motion or his grip is faulty. This drill is designed to give the coach an excellent opportunity to check the catcher's grip, throwing rotation, arm action, and body balance.

PROPER ARM ACTION AND BALANCE DRILL

In this drill, the catchers should be paired up so that they face each other from a distance of 50 to 60 feet. The coach then instructs the catchers to throw from a kneeling position, back and forth, while emphasiing their grip, body balance, and proper rotation on the ball.

This drill is of particular value to the catcher who demonstrates poor balance when throwing. After throwing a few times from the kneeling position, he will find that he must adjust his body and develop proper balance or else he will be unable to throw without falling. A real test of balance is to move the catchers to a distance of 90 feet apart. From that distance, they will not only develop balance, but strong wrist and arm action as well.

BLOCKING LOW PITCHES DRILL

The catcher should wear all of his catching equipment for this drill because he will find it necessary to block the ball with his body, as well as with his mitt. In order to block low pitches, the catcher should stay low and move quickly to get in front of the pitch. Developing the correct technique for blocking low pitches is less difficult if the coach specifies the direction of the throw. Such an approach will enable the catcher to concentrate on the proper mechanics of shifting. As the drill progresses, the catcher should learn to shift quickly by reacting to the ball. In this situation, he should not be forewarned about the direction of the throw. The catcher should be required to respond to and handle a variety of low throws. As such, these throws should bounce in front of him with varying degrees of speed and angle of bounce.

Two catchers may work together on this drill. To get maximum results, however, one of the catchers should designate himself as the thrower and the other as the receiver. This procedure allows time for the receiver to gather himself and get into his regular stance before receiving the next pitch. The catchers should be approximately 60 feet apart.

As is the case with most drills, results are more quickly attained if the coach throws the ball and points out the correct technique. If the coach throws the ball, he may wish to throw to one catcher and have the other catchers simulate the catch. In that case, the catchers should form a line facing the coach, at arm's length apart. They should execute the necessary footwork and body position on each throw. In this variation of the drill, the catchers must be told the direction of the throw.

BLOCKING LOW PITCHES AND RETRIEVING PASSED BALLS DRILL

This drill can be conducted in a number of ways. However, to make the drill resemble a game situation, it is best to put a runner on third base, a pitcher on the mound, and the catcher in full catching gear. Either the coach or one of the pitchers should then throw the ball in the dirt in front of the catcher. If the pitch gets by the catcher, the runner should break for the plate. If the catcher successfully blocks the pitch, the runner should remain at third base. If the ball gets by the catcher, he must retrieve it and throw it to the pitcher at home plate, who attempts to tag the runner.

This drill is designed to provide the catcher with the opportunity to work on low pitches and to practice quickly recovering balls that cannot be stopped. In retrieving passed balls, he should properly align himself with the target and then move so that he is open or in line with the target when he fields the ball. The catcher's alignment with the plate is particularly important on the passed ball that rolls in back of him and to his left. In that instance, he should make sure that when he picks up the ball, his left side is facing toward the target so that he will be in a good throwing position. As he runs to retrieve the ball, his back should be toward the infield. As such, he should approach the ball by keeping it to his left.

The catcher should use the same technique in fielding passed balls that he uses when fielding bunts. Accordingly, he should pick the ball up with both hands and should always align himself properly with the target.

THE CHALLENGE DRILL

This drill is designed to help the catcher block pitches in the dirt. However, before being introduced to this drill, the catchers should already have been taught the proper fundamentals and techniques of blocking low pitches. In this drill, the catchers' skills and endurance are challenged.

At least two catchers are necessary to operate the drill, but four is the ideal number. The drill requires that the catchers wear their gear, and that they assume their catcher's stance in the dirt area near home plate. The coach, who is on the mound, places a catcher on either side of him; who act as shaggers and partners for the active catchers.

The coach begins the drill by throwing pitches in the dirt to each catcher. Each catcher blocks the pitch, retrieves it before it stops rolling, and throws it to his partner, who feeds the ball to the coach. If the catcher does not block the ball, retrieve it before it stops rolling, or does not keep the ball out in front of him, his blocking duties are terminated at that point. After his turn has been completed, his partner announces the number of balls he successfully blocked, and then the two trade places. Each catcher is allowed only one turn.

What constitutes a successfully blocked ball is one that is either caught, or blocked with the mitt or any part of the catcher's body, and is also kept in front of him. It is important that the catcher not allow the ball to get past him. To help himself in this regard, he must make sure that the ball does not pass an imaginary line—a line that is even with the catcher's shoulders and parallel to the pitching rubber. If the ball is blocked and kept in front of this line, the catcher must retrieve it before it stops rolling.

This is an agility drill that requires that the catcher get in front of the ball, using his hands and body properly, and make a quick recovery to retrieve the ball. At the end of the drill, the coach should declare one of his catchers the champion. To add a degree of competition to the drill, it is up to the others to beat him the next time they take part in the drill.

SHORT HOP DRILL

The purpose of this drill is to improve the catcher's level of hand-eye coordination. The catchers should pair off and face each other about 30 to 40 feet apart and make short-hop throws to one another. Each catcher must try to keep his eyes on the ball and, at the same time, keep his hands low and relaxed so that he can move quickly to the ball. Each catcher should try to make his throws difficult for his partner to catch.

If the catcher keeps his mitt low and well out in front of his body, his ability to field these short-hop throws will improve in time. This drill is designed to accentuate the position and use of the catcher's mitt.

POP FLY DRILL

Although pop-fly drills may be conducted anywhere on the field, the best area to perform this drill is the home ground of the catcher, home plate. When pop-fly drills are conducted around home plate, the catcher can develop a sound knowledge of how the ball rotates in relation to home plate. He also learns how to catch fly balls near the screen and dugouts. In other words, he learns how much area he can cover successfully.

When performing this drill, the catcher should always wear his catching equipment whenever feasible. Such a practice will enable him to become better accustomed to his equipment and will also allow him to learn how to remove and properly discard his mask. After he discards his mask, the catcher must be sure to pick it up before the next pop fly is hit so he can avoid injury. Since the catcher's routine of continually taking off his mask during this drill would be time-consuming, the coach may choose to have the catcher practice this drill without his equipment. However, if the coach decides to have the catcher wear his gear, the extra time that needs to be devoted to this drill will pay off down the road.

To make this drill resemble a game situation as much as possible, the catcher should assume his catching stance with his head down. Upon hearing the bat strike the ball, he should immediately try to locate the ball. During a real game, the catcher normally does not see the foul ball come off the bat. As a result, by keeping his head down, he is creating a situation similar to what he will encounter on a foul pop throughout the season.

A good deal of practice is necessary to learn how to catch pop flies. The spin of the baseball plays havoc with the catcher who is inexperienced. In reality, the only way for him to gain experience in catching pop flies is through trial and error. This drill needs to be repeated until the catcher has successfully mastered the ability to catch pop flies. This skill is one of those attributes that require lots of time and repetition.

POP FLY WITH CATCHER ASSISTING FIRST AND THIRD BASEMEN DRILL

The purpose of this drill is to help the catcher develop the habit of assisting his fellow players on pop flies. The catcher, third baseman, and first baseman may all be used in this drill. Each player involved in the drill should assume his normal playing position. When the pop fly is hit, the catcher should move in the direction of the ball, as should the first or third baseman, depending on which side of the infield the ball is hit. If one of the other fielders field the ball, the catcher should move away from the play, but remain in line with the ball and in view of the player to verbally and visually assist him. If the catcher stays in line with, but clear of, the ball, the baseman can use him as a guide. If the ball is near the screen or dugout, the catcher should move directly to that area and place his hand on the object and yell warnings to the fielder, telling him that he either has plenty of room or is getting very close to the impediment. Of course, the first baseman and third baseman should reciprocate when the catcher fields the ball.

Many balls can be fielded near obstructions if the players involved work together to help each other. Even while looking up at the pop fly, the fielder who has a play on the ball is able to get a glimpse of teammate who is going to assist him. If the player has his hand on the fence or dugout, the fielder will see this and know that he must move with caution. On the other hand, if the assisting player is standing away from the impediment, the fielder will know that he can be more aggressive in his efforts to get the ball.

It is important that every fielder is previously well schooled individually on pop flies before the coach employs this particular drill. If one of the players involved has too much difficulty in catching the pop fly, he will be in the way of the other players and actually be a danger to them. Since one of the major purposes of this drill is to prevent injuries, using an unschooled player in this situation would certainly be counterproductive.

RHYTHM DRILL

The purpose of this drill is for the catcher to develop a proper sense of rhythm in his throwing. To develop this skill, the catcher must first learn to shift his weight smoothly. After receiving the pitch, he must properly grip the ball and clear himself from the batter, all the while maintaining his balance.

Because good rhythm and balance enhance the ability of a catcher to throw accurately, it is vital that the catcher learn to coordinate all of his movements if he is to indeed develop rhythm. Rhythm not only helps the catcher get his throws away quickly, but adds to his consistency as well. Furthermore, rhythmical throw is also less taxing on the arm.

The catcher can either practice this drill while wearing his gear, or he can choose not to. However, the catcher should keep in mind that in all of his drills, he should wear his equipment enough to enable him to become accustomed to it.

In this drill, one of the catchers acts as a hitter, while another catcher takes his regular position behind the plate. If the drill involves a third catcher, he should move to second base, where he should anticipate receiving a throw. On the other hand, if the number of catchers is limited, an infielder should be called in to cover second base. The coach should position himself on the mound and should begin the drill by throwing to the catcher behind the plate, indicating the direction in which the ball will be thrown. It should be noted that it is generally a good idea on all drills of this type to indicate the direction of the throw, because this information enables the catcher to concentrate on executing the proper mechanics for moving in that particular direction and also helps him develop his confidence. As the catcher's confidence and ability grow, he will learn to shift automatically to the pitch and will not need to be told where the ball is going to be thrown.

As the coach delivers his first pitch, the catcher, on the count of one, should step to and catch the pitch. On two, he should bring the ball up into the throwing position and clear himself from the batter. On three, he should complete this rhythmic process by throwing the ball to second base. The catcher should go through each phase of his throwing motion at the same speed. The speed at which he will operate will depend on his own ability. It should be noted that speed, in this instance, is not as important here as continuity. The catcher's entire motion must be fluid and rhythmical, with no hesitation at any point.

In this drill, the catcher should also practice his footwork and work on clearing from the hitter, gripping the ball properly, and throwing. Considering the workout he will get, this exercise is probably the best all-around drill the catcher can perform.

COVERING THIRD BASE ON BUNTS DRILL

On any ball that forces the third baseman to move in toward home plate, the catcher should move toward third base and be ready to cover the bag. Toward that end, this drill is an excellent way to remind the catcher of his responsibilities for covering third base on bunts because it consists of hitting slow rollers to the third baseman. As the ball is fielded, the catcher should direct the third baseman where to throw the ball. As the two players pass each other, the catcher should also remind the third baseman that he will cover his base. If the third baseman is able to get back and cover the bag, he should do so. Obviously, proper communication between the two players is important. All factors considered, the best way to develop good communication is through committed practice.

DRILL FOR BLOCKING THE PLATE DRILL

This drill can be conducted either with or without the catcher's gear. If runners are used in this drill, however, it will be necessary for the catcher to wear his equipment. In this drill, all of the outfielders are placed in the outfield, where they can field ground balls and throw to the plate. The catcher, meanwhile, should position himself approximately two full steps behind home plate, directly facing the outfielder who is fielding the ball and throwing to him. As the throw approaches the plate, the catcher should judge the bounce of the ball and move to make the catch. This method encourages the catcher to move into, rather than away from, the ball.

The same type of drill may be used with the infielders making the throws. When the infielders throw the ball, however, the catcher should put himself in a tagging position. Throws from infielders are normally thrown without a bounce. Therefore, no need exists for the catcher to move into the throw.

FUNGOES FROM THE OUTFIELD TO THE CATCHER DRILL

The catcher never seems to get enough throws from his outfielders. That situation is particularly unfortunate, because the catcher's ability to handle these throws during the game can be crucial. Since time constraints during practice prevent outfielders from making enough throws to accommodate their catcher, a good alternative is to have a fungo man hit fungoes from the outfield to the catcher. Although not exactly the same as a long throw, the long fungo hit is similar enough to be useful under these circumstances.

The primary purpose of this drill is to give the catcher the opportunity to learn to read the rotation and hop of the ball, a situation that is deisgned to give him a chance to adjust to the skip of the ball off the grass. In addition, this drill is a good opportunity for the catcher to practice the tag play.

During this drill, several balls should be hit from each of the outfield positions, from a distance of 220 feet to 250 feet. The fungo man should try to hit a one-hop bounce to the catcher, although some balls will bounce more than once, and some will carry all the way to the catcher on the fly. Since a catcher must deal with all kinds of throws in the game, this drill can provide him with a wide variety of simulated throws. The catcher should practice this drill in full gear, including his mask. He should also wear his mask when taking outfield throws during games.

FIELDING BUNTS DRILL

This drill is a very simple, yet very important exercise-one that the catchers may undertake by themselves. One catcher should station himself at the base to which the throw is to be delivered, while the other catcher should start behind home plate with a ball that he rolls a short distance in front of the plate. He then moves out quickly, aligns himself properly, fields the ball, and throws to the base. This drill should be also involve having the catcher field balls both behind and to the side of him so that he will become accustomed to fielding passed balls and retrieving and throwing them. The catcher should practice throwing to each base.

The catcher should remember to always use both hands when he fields a bunted ball, so that both his mitt and his bare hand can close in on the ball. By using both hands, the catcher is able to get the proper grip on the ball as he brings it into the throwing position. He then pushes the ball against his mitt as sets his grip. The mitt not only helps the catcher pick up the ball, but it also helps him employ the proper grip.

PICKOFF DRILL

The pickoff drill affords the catcher the opportunity to practice his footwork, as well as his throwing mechanics on pickoff plays. In this drill, a batter should be stationed at home plate to best simulate a game situation. The drill begins when a pitcher or a coach throws to the catcher from the mound. The catcher should receive the ball, using the proper footwork in the process, and then clear himself from the batter and throw to the designated base. Beginning catchers should throw directly overhand. As they progress, they should practice throwing sidearm to first base. Sidearm throws are not as powerful as overhand throws, but they are more deceptive and can be delivered quickly. To its credit, however, the overhand throw is more accurate and can be completed just as quickly. It should be noted that some catchers are accurate and very quick with the sidearm delivery, while others are erratic. As always, the player should use the method that works best for him.

FORCED PLAYS AT HOME PLATE DRILL

The purpose of this drill is to give the catcher practice at tagging home plate on forceouts and double plays. At the outset of the drill, all of the infielders should be in their respective positions. The coach initiates the drill by hitting a ground ball to each infielder, who then throws the ball directly to the catcher, who in turn steps on home plate and throws to first base.

As the drill progresses, the same procedure should again be employed, but this time with the second baseman and the shortstop back in a deep fielding position. With one out and the bases loaded, the shortstop and second baseman are normally required to attempt the double play at second base. They do not throw to home plate from the deep position on ordinary plays. Meanwhile, the first and third basemen are both playing shallow. If the ball is hit to either of them in such a manner that it forces movement toward second base, then their throw should be made to that base. However, if the ball goes straight to the fielder, he should throw to the catcher, who should step on home plate and throw to first base for a double play.

On this play, the catcher should incorporate the arm fake to first base, followed by a throw to third base. If no chance exists to get a double play, the catcher should opt to use the arm fake to first base and then throw to third base. This drill is designed to help the catcher learn when to use this particular play. If the normal timing of the play is disrupted, the fake throw may be appropriate. Usually, the normal timing is broken by a bobbled ball, a delay in getting rid of the ball, or an unusual hop. A number of other factors should be considered as well. For example, an exceptionally fast runner, or one who gets a great jump from third base, may force the catcher to opt for the fake move.

DEVELOPING SKILLS BY CATCHING BATTING PRACTICE

Catching batting practice can either be a beneficial activity or a waste of valuable time. On one hand, it can be employed to help to improve the catcher's skills, while on the other hand, or it can serve as a dull, boring activity of little value. During batting practice, many catchers merely station themselves behind the plate and do little more than stop the ball and throw it back to the batting practice pitcher. To their credit, other players wisely use this time to work on their catching skills.

One suggestion that may add to the development of the catcher's skills is to outline the duties required of the catcher at the start of batting practice. If the catcher follows this outline, he will find that catching for batting practice can be a valuable and interesting experience. He will discover that it is a good time for him to try to improve in those areas where he is weak. He may choose, for example, to concentrate on any or all of the following tasks: catching the ball with relaxed hands; improving his footwork and rhythm; clearing from the batter; gripping the ball properly; blocking low pitches; or throwing. Setting a goal or establishing a purpose in catching batting practice provides one of the best learning situations for the catcher.

A wise catcher develops a plan during batting practice. A portion of batting practice can be done in a relaxed manner, while another segment can consist of drills that are accomplished with game–like precision. The time in batting practice should be executed with game-like timing. A good plan calls for the catcher to alternate his routine. He should, for instance, designate a prescribed number of pitches for a period of time when he can work on specific fundamentals. The major part of batting practice, however, can be caught in a relaxed manner.

Since the catcher should be thought of as the leader of the team, he should display his leadership during batting practice by helping to keep the practice running smoothly. He should count the swings each batter takes to make sure all take an equal number; he should also remind his teammates to alternate quickly when retrieving batted and thrown balls.

THE CATCHER'S RESPONSIBILITIES DURING INFIELD WARM-UPS

Because the catcher is visible to all his teammates, his attitude is extremely important. A catcher who exhibits eagerness and desire shows his teammates the type of attitude he expects in return. If he is easily discouraged and frustrated, his teammates will likely demonstrate a similar attitude. Accordingly, it is the duty of the catcher to set a good example by hustling at all times and encouraging his teammates to follow his example.

Like batting practice, infield warm-ups can be excellent learning situations with great carryover value, or they can be prove to be poor learning situations with little or no carryover value. Many catchers, for example, stand in front of home plate during infield warm-ups, take throws in an upright position, and throw without using proper footwork. For this type of player, it is doubtful that this type of warm-up has any carryover value at all.

During warm-ups, the catcher should receive throws from his regular catching position behind home plate and should face the pitching rubber as he would in a game. Even though most of his footwork is initiated by throws made by the first baseman, the catcher should still receive these throws while facing the pitching rubber. This habit will encourage him to use the proper footwork.

During infield practice, the catcher should place an imaginary batter at home plate and then practice his footwork with that hitter in mind. His imaginary hitter should be right-handed during one round of infield practice and left-handed during another. By alternating this way, the catcher will have plenty of opportunities to work on his footwork and rhythm. For players who adhere to these procedures, no doubt exists that this type of infield practice will have some carryover value. As a result, the coach should be emphasize that the catcher should stay behind home plate and simulate a game situation on each throw he receives during warm-ups.

THE CATCHER'S RESPONSIBILITY IN WARMING UP PITCHERS

One of the most important duties of the catcher is to warm up the pitcher. It is during this daily workout that the catcher can be a big help to the pitcher by maintaining a positive attitude during this warm-up period. If a throw from the pitcher is low and bounces off the ground and hits the catcher, the catcher's reaction should not be disgust and anger; rather it should reflect concern and, subsequently, encouragement to

the pitcher. Catching for pitchers requires both stamina and patience. This time period should also give the catcher an opportunity to find something good in what the pitcher is doing or, on the other hand, provide him with grounds to offer the pitcher constructive criticism.

The catcher should always be alert to any unusual movement the ball may take and be ready to immediately relay that information to the pitcher. Often the pitcher will experiment with different grips, in an attempt to get better movement on his pitch. When he does, a catcher's encouragement, appraisal, and alertness may subsequently help the pitcher improve or develop a particular pitch.

By the same token, a lack of enthusiasm by the catcher will make it difficult for the pitcher to concentrate on his pitching skills. If the catcher complains when the pitcher throws hard; or when a wild pitch is thrown, the pitcher may lose his concentration. If he does, and the warm-up will end up having little value. The catcher should remember that he is there to help the pitcher.

A pitcher with great movement is often hard to catch. Therefore, the catcher needs to upgrade his own skills rather than ask the pitcher to take movement off his pitch to make it easier to catch. The wild pitcher, of course, needs encouragement, and a catcher who accepts the challenge of helping this pitcher throw with more accuracy will often have a big impact on that pitcher's level of control and effectiveness. If the pitcher is unusually wild, or throws pitches that are difficult to catch, the catcher should wear his catching gear during the warm-up for added security.

CHAPTER 5

Psychological Implications and Concepts of Strategy

On the surface, the outcome of a baseball game is determined by the performance of the players on a given day. What is often overlooked, however, are the psychological factors that affect the abilities of the players. In some situations, these factors have helped turn a sure loser into a surprise winner and vice-versa. How many times, for instance, have fans seen a pitcher lose his control and load the bases, only to be let off the hook by his shortstop, who turns a sensational unassisted double play? How about the catcher who kills a rally by picking the running off of first base? In both cases, the pitcher is often so spurred on by the shift in momentum that he regains his effectiveness and goes on to chalk up the victory. So much of the game of baseball is mental that it is important for the coach to be aware of the psychological implications of those events that occur maybe once, sometimes several times, during the course of a ball game.

Some managers and coaches are masterful at dealing with the mental aspects of a team. They are able to motivate their players because they recognize what causes letdowns and what creates competitive fervor. Consequently, these coaches also realize what they have to say and do in order to have a positive influence on their team's state of mind.

The on-field extension of the manager or coach is the catcher, who the players look to for signal calling and leadership. Because he is involved with every pitch of the game, the catcher is the player whose actions can most affect his teammates. Accordingly, the catcher must also understand the psychological implications of key plays so that he can motivate the other players.

Many coaches feel that it is possible for a winning team to have one or two players who do not possess an outward show of aggressiveness, but the catcher must not be one of them. The catcher may lack ability, but he should not lack determination and desire. He may not be a talker, either, but as long as he is aggressive, forceful, and demanding, he will motivate his teammates by exhibiting a quiet, positive, confident attitude.

PITCHER-CATCHER RAPPORT

A good pitcher controls the game because he is the one with the ball in his hand, and the action does not begin until he delivers it to the plate. Since it is widely accepted that a team's success or failure is dependent on the ability of its pitching staff, it is essential that the pitcher establish an excellent rapport with the everyday team leader–the catcher. After all, it is one thing to baffle a hitter; it is quite another to baffle your catcher. In a baseball sense, it is a tragedy to have a catcher who is constantly crossed up by his own pitcher. A team beset with this problem is unable to capitalize on its assets, because its strengths must be curtailed in order to compensate for its weaknesses. If, on the other hand, the catcher lacks talent and leadership qualities, the pitcher will be forced to reduce his ability level to match the ability level of the catcher. It does little good, for example, to strike out the batter, only to have the catcher charged with a passed ball that enables the batter to reach first base. It is also troublesome to have runners advance on similarly mishandled pitches by the catcher.

A catcher should be able to successfully catch the best pitch that each pitcher can throw. Even in the major leagues, however, such is not always the case. Some catchers, for instance, are not adept at fielding low pitches. As a result, the pitcher may be forced to throw his pitches slightly higher than the game strategy would otherwise indicate. In crucial situations, this adjustment is often disastrous, because the pitcher is likely to lose his effectiveness and get knocked around. The long-term consequences of poor catching do not bode well for team unity. At the least, it can destroy the relationship between the pitcher and the catcher.

The first step in establishing rapport between the battery mates should be made by the catcher. However, a good relationship between the two is dependent upon input from both parties. The catcher initiates the relationship by becoming a part of the pitcher's performance. He does this by using common sense–based on the understanding that almost anyone will respond positively when another person shows concern for him. It is precisely this concern and empathy, therefore, that the catcher needs to show to each of his pitchers. A catcher who hustles and takes care of his own position usually has the respect of his pitching staff. Pitchers appreciate and revere the work of a good catcher.

Not only should a catcher be conscientious about catching the ball, he must also concentrate on ways to help his pitcher. Perhaps more than any other player, the catcher is required to show more interest in the pitcher than in himself. A catcher who is loyal to his pitchers will generously be repaid with respect from the pitcher. By making each pitcher feel special, and by contributing input and interest on a daily basis, the catcher will gain the confidence and respect of each pitcher. As such, virtually every pitching activity during practice should involve the catcher.

In building their rapport, the pitcher and the catcher should first lay out a few ground rules. It will help immensely if the catcher adheres to the following guidelines:

- Get involved. Pay attention to what is going on. Listen to the coach's instructions to the pitcher. If the pitcher is trying to improve his fundamentals, become a part of that process.

- Show interest in the pitcher. Care enough to both compliment and criticize the pitcher as appropriate. The pitcher will respond well to both positive and negative feedback if the catcher truly shows an interest in him.

- Be aggressive. The pitcher will appreciate a catcher who hustles, because it is infectious and tends to help the whole team rise to the occasion.

- Be enthusiastic. The trademark of a doer is enthusiasm. If the catcher is enthusiastic during practice as well as games, he will make repetitious drills seem a lot more fun than they would be if he showed little spark.

- Encourage pitchers with positive actions and words. The catcher should always display a positive demeanor, even when he is criticizing the pitcher. His primary goal should be to help the pitcher achieve positive results. Positive words turn on others' power source, and they lead to positive action.

- Avoid complaining. Complaining and whining send negative messages to the pitcher and the rest of the team and also suggest that there are no solutions to the problems that exist. By complaining, the catcher, in effect, is begging for an easy way out of a particular situation. Instead, the catcher needs to look at a problem as a challenge. In fact, he should look at every problem as something he can handle.

- Cooperate. The catcher should be willing to catch a few extra pitches when asked. He should also be willing to listen to suggestions from each pitcher, just as he would expect the pitcher to listen to his own suggestions. Although cooperation is vital if a catcher is to have a good rapport with the pitcher, he must not become subservient; rather, he must remember to cooperate from the position of being a leader.

- Be assertive. Because the catcher's decisions are often critical to the team's welfare, he cannot afford to be timid. If he is reliable, makes sound judgments, and takes charge, his teammates will respond positively to him.

- Treat each pitcher with respect. Again, the catcher's common sense and understanding of human nature can do wonders for any pitcher. Accordingly, the catcher should show the pitcher that he respects him and that he in turn expects the pitcher to reciprocate.

As a leader, the catcher must be cooperative and willing to help, but he should not allow the pitcher to take advantage of him. He needs the pitcher to be held accountable for his own set of guidelines:

- Have a purpose. The pitcher should carry over his predetermined purpose from practice to games. He needs to be responsible for his game plan and let the catcher know what his goals are. In turn, the catcher will be better able to help the pitcher achieve his goals.

- Be aggressive. In order to improve, a pitcher must be willing to endure repetitious drills. If he exhibits aggressiveness in those drills, he will send a positive message to the catcher and the rest of the team and will also be more likely to realize positive results.

- Cooperate. One small detail may make a major difference in a pitch or some part of the delivery. A cooperative pitcher who is willing to take advice often picks up details that will help his game. Accordingly, the pitcher should become a sponge for knowledge. He should listen and learn and be willing to make adjustments. At the same time, however, he should be smart enough to know when and why he should make these necessary adjustments.

- Avoid complaining. If the pitcher reacts negatively to problems, it follows that he will have difficulty solving them. Problems are there to be solved. Complaining only serves to exacerbate a particular proble. Furthermore, it tends to demonstrate to others that the pitcher cannot be a problem solver. In short, it projects an image of failure.

  The pitcher must remember to substitute a solution for every possible complaint he might have had, and he should follow up by taking whatever time is necessary to come up with the appropriate solution.

- Practice and play with poise. It is easier to be poised when things are going your way. Thus, when a pitcher finds himself in a pressure-packed situation, the poise he shows should indicate strength, determination, and commitment. Poise is a quality that the pitcher should wear on his face and have in his heart during practices, as well as games.

- Be willing to fix things. The pitcher should constantly be mending, repairing. He needs to be making adjustments as he goes. It is these adjustments that will, in the end, help him fully develop his pitching skills. However, once he reaches the point where he has sufficiently honed his skills, he must be vigilant about maintaining those skills.

- Look like a winner. The pitcher's body language is important. If he hangs his head or droops his shoulders, he will appear uncertain and defeatist. On the other hand, if he holds his head high and has a fierce, competitive look on his face, he will look like a winner.

Although the catcher has other responsibilities, his major assignment is to assist the pitcher. From handling bullpen duties to providing leadership during the game, the catcher can find many ways to help. Despite the availability of tools and gimmicks that the catcher can use to help the pitcher, it is really his savvy and encouragement that are typically have the greatest impact on the pitcher. The catcher, for example, can give any target that a commercial target screen offers. Unlike the commercial target, however, the catcher motivates and evaluates. The catcher's range of assistance has no boundaries. He may help the pitcher with information on his mechanics, or he may merely help the pitcher stay focused. Through concern and interest, the catcher can impart worthwhile suggestions to the pitcher. It is the responsibility of the pitcher to listen to that advice.

The catcher should develop the attitude that he can help any pitcher As such, he should project this attitude to the entire pitching staff. By developing the tools to communicate and gathering as much information as possible on the art of pitching, as well as his insights into his own pitchers, the catcher can help each pitcher maximize his effort.

The bullpen is the center of the work place for the pitcher and the catcher. It should be their special place. Again, both battery mates should adhere to certain guidelines:

For example, they should never enter the bullpen without a plan. The pitcher should have a specific goal for each workout, and this plan should be revealed to the catcher before any pitches are thrown. Since both of them are responsible for seeing that the plan is carried out, it is important that the pitcher and the catcher remain focused on the job at hand. Although it is often difficult to stay focused when something goes wrong (e.g., the pitcher cannot find his curveball), the catcher can minimize the impact of such a distraction by using his powers of persuasion to settle down the pitcher. Once he calms the pitcher, the catcher should then try to keep him focused on the daily bullpen goal.

Since the pitcher's moods will play a big role in his practice habits, the catcher should remain enthusiastic, even during bullpen drills. Enthusiasm uplifts and excites, and it is the key to a good learning environment. Accordingly, before entering the bullpen, the pitcher and the catcher should evaluate their state of mind. They should ensure that their mental approach is relatively satisfactory before undertaking a bullpen workout.

The catcher's success in the bullpen is largely dependent upon his ability to tune in and evaluate the pitcher's fundamentals. For example, a good catcher notices the rotation of each pitch. He can also tell whether the pitcher's delivery is consistent, or even if the pitcher's level of intensity has diminished. A good catcher also notices when a pitcher has lapsed into sloppy work habits and works with him to get him back up to speed.

The major purpose of the bullpen workout is simple: for the pitcher to improve. As such, the catcher can help the pitcher by encouraging him to work hard to get from one point to the next, until the pitcher achieves his long-term goals. It is up to the catcher to make sure that the pitcher meets the prescribed standard of excellence.

Bullpen practice also affords the pitcher the opportunity to refine, or sharpen, his skills. However, refinement is not an easy task. It takes a very keen eye and a good deal of skill. In attempting to refine a curveball, for instance, in terms of making improvement, the pitcher often finds that a slight adjustment, rather than drastic measures, will do the trick. Overexuberance by the pitcher and catcher, on the other hand, could result in serious setbacks. As a consequence, they should keep in mind that they are not working on building a new engine; the already sound engine just needs a simple tune-up. Therefore, if maintenance is the reason for the workout, the pitcher and catcher should not attempt to make any changes. They should, however, expect that the pitcher's level of skill matches the highest possible standards. Bullpen practice is not just a workout, because the pitcher is already highly skilled. Accordingly, each of his pitches should be thrown with that in mind. A pitcher working on maintenance should be sharp and concise and should avoid becoming sloppy or taking things for granted. Attaining success is difficult. Remaining successful is often even harder.

The bullpen workout should run smoothly. All factors considered, it will if the pitcher and catcher cooperate with one another. Cooperation encourages everyone to chip in and help.

Often, catchers try to find excuses not to have to catch in the bullpen. After all, such work is tiring. However, it can be very rewarding as well, as long as the catcher accepts the challenge with a positive attitude. If the catcher shows enthusiasm, he will help transform the bullpen from a dull desert into an exciting oasis.

With regard to making bullpen practice a meaningful experience, it will help tremendously if the pitcher and the catcher adhere to certain guidelines:

- Go into the bullpen with a plan:
    - be enthusiastic.
    - be aware of details.

- improve, refine, or maintain.
- cooperate.
- avoid negative behavior.
- make it exciting.

As he builds his rapport with the pitcher, the catcher may find that there are many other ways to earn the respect of the pitching staff. One of the most effective ways to get close to the pitcher and gain his confidence is to coax him with positive words and phrases, such as "you can get better" instead of "you have to get better." By using positive words, the catcher can not only implore the pitcher to improve, but also leave him with a feeling of self-worth. Since many pitchers lack confidence, it is important that the catcher be aware of this fact so that he can communicate his advice and, at the same time, help instill confidence in the pitcher.

Body language also speaks volumes. Accordingly, the catcher must be aware of what he is saying with his body. Often, the statements he makes with his body language are devastating to the pitcher. For example, when a pitcher throws a good a pitch but gets poor results, the catcher's reaction may be critical to the pitcher's level of success throughout the rest of the game.

The catcher should get well acquainted with each pitcher. As such, he should be able to read him like a book. He should know what excites, pressures, and motivates each pitcher. Of course, in order to know the pitcher, he has to spend time with him—and there is no better time spent than the time spent in the bullpen.

A good knowledge of the pitcher's personality traits is valuable to the catcher. Each pitcher has a unique personality and that tends to make him react differently to certain game situations. Some pitchers, for instance, have a tendency to relax and become careless. If the catcher understands this trait in a particular individual, his persistent and forceful suggestions may help the pitcher to concentrate. Other pitchers tense up in crucial situations. These players may be helped by a catcher who is able to momentarily distract them with a joke or a discussion of a topic that is completely unrelated to the game. If the catcher succeeds in relaxing the pitcher, and is able to motivate him with positive words and thoughts, the pitcher will likely regain his confidence and his ability to instill fear in the opposing team.

Another key ingredient to building rapport with the pitcher is the catcher's total support of the pitcher. By placing the pitcher's performance and needs ahead of his own personal goals, the catcher will also be showing the pitcher and the team that he is putting the team ahead of his own ego. In the end, however, it really is up to the catcher to assume the full responsibility for initiating rapport with the pitcher.

PITCHER-CATCHER CONFERENCES

Fans and observers of the game of baseball often wonder what it is that the pitcher and the catcher talk about when the catcher trots out to the mound for a conference. Some believe that psychological warfare takes place during these talks, while others maintain that these conferences serve only to relieve the pitcher's tension.

Actually, no set rules exist or procedures for the catcher or the pitcher to follow during these conferences. The catcher may want to discuss game strategy, talk about fundamentals, go over signs, or even give the pitcher a rest. Often, the purpose of the conference is to try to change the pitcher's mood in order to get him to concentrate better. Regardless of the reason, however, the catcher must make sure that the conference is in harmony with the game situation and the pitcher's attitude.

If the pitcher appears tense and anxious, the catcher may feel that it is appropriate to interrupt his concentration by discussing something other than the game. On the other hand, the catcher may sense that the situation calls for added concentration on the part of the pitcher. In this case, he may remind the pitcher of the gravity of the situation and assure him that by concentrating and putting forth his best effort, a successful result will follow. The catcher must know the personality of the pitcher and use the approach that best suits that player's unique personality. Under stress, some pitchers respond well to suggestions, while others do not. For example, the catcher must know when to compliment and when to challenge. Sometimes the best medicine is laughter; other times, it is silence. The key is that the catcher should understand what makes the pitcher tick in order to determine what approach will work best in a particular situation.

PITCHING CHANGES INVOLVING THE CATCHERS

The catcher is frequently called upon to advise the coach about the effectiveness of the pitcher, often in the presence of the pitcher. Despite the fact that some catchers feel that these situations threaten their rapport with the pitcher, that should not be a problem if the two have already developed an honest and meaningful relationship. In these instances, the catcher should be able to truthfully appraise the pitcher's effectiveness without damaging his relationship with the pitcher.

The catcher has an obligation to the team and to the pitcher. If the pitcher becomes ineffective, the catcher should not hesitate to tell the coach. Furthermore, and he should not feel that he needs to apologize to anyone. His evaluation should be honest and to the point. He should keep in mind that he should avoid placing blame on the pitcher (i.e., just the facts...no blame).

On many occasions the catcher will be in a position to give a positive evaluation of the pitcher's effectiveness. Over a complete season, the positive and negative evaluations will probably cancel each other out. If all concerned parties are made to realize that such evaluations are honest and sincere, the catcher's judgment can be of immeasurable value to everyone involved.

CATCHER-UMPIRE RELATIONSHIP

In order for the umpire to accurately determine balls and strikes on marginal pitches, he must have a clear view of each pitch. The catcher can help both his pitcher and the umpire by providing a good view of the action for the umpire. Unfortunately, many catchers have a habit of standing up on some pitches. This regrettable action often causes the umpire to either guess where the pitch crossed the plate or, more likely, to call the pitch a ball. Accordingly, using a low stance and remaining low while fielding pitches is of great assistance to the umpire. The catcher should always be helpful in giving the umpire a good view, so that the umpire will be able to do a better job at calling pitches.

Most umpires are very conscientious and sincerely try to call each pitch correctly. Some tend to miss certain pitches. Occasionally, the umpire will be inconsistent on pitches in a certain location. The catcher should keep in mind that umpires are like players. They come in all sizes and different personalities and abilities. In order to understand the umpire and to adjust to how he is calling the game, it is a good idea to get to know him. If good rapport is established by the catcher at the outset, both the catcher and the umpire can profit.

Very few umpires make a bad call on purpose. Because they're human, all of them make mistakes, however. Most umpires sincerely want to do a good job, but pressure and tension affect them much the same way these factors affect the players. It should be remembered that umpires are all very different. Each responds to given situations in his own way. It is imperative that the catcher get acquainted with the umpire and get the hang of his strike zone.

The catcher should begin to establish the proper relationship with the umpire by showing respect, by being congenial, and by being honest. If the proper atmosphere exists, the umpire will not become offended when the catcher suggests that the umpire has made a mistake on a pitch. Of course, it is imperative that tact should be used at all times. The catcher should be quick to praise the umpire when he makes an exceptionally good call, even if it is not in the catcher's favor. The catcher should try to establish an atmosphere of honesty and sincerity with the umpire. A negative, begging, or nagging approach usually proves unsuccessful and generally leads to a tense and cautious relationship.

No attempt should be made to trick or fool the umpire. Such an approach will only serve to antagonize the umpire and result in mistrust and hard feelings. The catcher should not expect, or seek, to have bad pitches called strikes. If the pitch is called a ball, but is very close to being a strike, the catcher should assure the umpire that the pitch has been called properly. On the other hand, if the pitch is close, but was a strike, and the umpire has called it a ball, the catcher should indicate, respectfully, that the umpire has missed the pitch. If this approach is properly followed, most umpires will place a value on the catcher's judgment, and the catcher will earn the umpire's respect

The catcher should realize that even good umpires make a few mistakes on balls and strikes during the course of a game. The catcher should not violently protest a call if it is the first call the umpire has missed. This act alone may set off an unfavorable relationship for the remainder of the game. However, the catcher should make it known that the pitch was not properly called.

If a difference of opinion concerning a pitch exists, the disagreement should be between only the catcher and the umpire. There should be no attempt to embarrass or antagonize the umpire, and when talking to him, the catcher should face the pitcher. Turning around to discuss a pitch with the umpire is unwise. This act shows the fans and players that the catcher disagrees with the umpire. As such, it also invites booing and harassment of the umpire.

The catcher may solidify a working relationship with the umpire by encouraging his teammates, especially the pitcher, to refrain from questioning close calls on balls and strikes. It must be made clear that the catcher is to do the talking on all close pitches.

The primary reason for the catcher to establish a good relationship with the umpire is that it is the right thing to do. This insight is not to say the catcher has more concern about the umpire than he has for his pitcher. He should fight for his pitcher. The umpire, meanwhile, should be aware that the catcher and the pitcher are both competitive and want to win.

An honest appraisal of the pitch is always the best policy for the catcher to pursue. If, for instance, the coach questions a close call by the umpire, the catcher should be honest enough to indicate whether the pitch was a ball or a strike, regardless of the game situation. After calling a close pitch, the umpire will often question the catcher about the validity of the call. On such occasions, the catcher should be perfectly frank, regardless of whether the call was favorable or unfavorable. If the catcher is honest, the umpire will more likely respond by having confidence in the catcher's opinions.

STRATEGY

Setting up a plan of attack involves physical and mental readiness. Since the pitcher and catcher play such an important role in team strategy, it is imperative that both attain a high level of physical conditioning. Physical fatigue brings on mental fatigue. A tired catcher is a careless thinker. In a similar view, a pitcher in poor physical condition is not as competitive as he should be. A tired pitcher lacks speed and control.

Strategy calls for the pitcher and the catcher to know the abilities of their own team, as well as the abilities of the opposing team. In other words, they must both match their skill and knowledge with the skill and knowledge of the opposition. The situation may call for strength against strength or strength against weakness. A good catcher makes sound decisions in this area.

The catcher plays a major role in developing and carrying out strategy. He must study his pitcher's skills and work habits, and he must study the skills and work habits of the opposition as well. The catcher should know the batters' weaknesses and strengths, which occasionally change during the course of a season. Accordingly, it is important that the catcher understand the ongoing nature of his responsibilities in this area and to make keen observations and collect and file his insights for future use.

The most important strategic factor is the pitcher's strength. The catcher should be aware of the pitcher's most effective pitch. He should know his own pitcher almost as well as he knows himself. In any given situation, the catcher should be able to match up with his pitcher's pitches. One situation may call for more breaking pitches; another may call for a number of fastballs. The pitcher and the catcher should be prepared for any occasion.

The pitcher and catcher should feel as though they have the advantage. In reality, they do, because they know how and where each pitch will be thrown. Accordingly, they can use control as their weapon. By throwing to certain parts of the strike zone, the pitcher can neutralize or even negate a hitter's strength. By spotting the ball, or by varying the placement of his deliveries, the pitcher can disrupt the batter's focus and set him up for the strikeout or weak grounder.

Strategy, of course, is always complicated by the presence of base-runners. The baserunners' intentions must be anticipated by the catcher, who needs to consider many factors when calling signals or preparing to make a play.

The pitcher's skill level is also a major factor in drawing up a game plan. The pitcher must know his capabilities. Furthermore, the catcher must also be aware of what the pitcher can and cannot do, and then guide him along the way. Ultimately, the pitcher and catcher must both be aware of the pitcher's best pitches in order to utilize those pitches in key situations in the game.

Adjustment to the elements is another important facet in overall planning for the game. If it is extremely windy, for example, the pitcher and catcher should try to use the wind to their advantage by making the appropriate adjustments and then incorporating those adjustments into their game plan.

The lighting, background, and layout of the field also may figure into the game plan. A poorly lighted ball park, for example, will play into the hands of a hard-throwing pitcher. A particular background, meanwhile, may favor a left-handed pitcher over a right-hander.

Indeed, all facilities at the ball park should be appraised and considered in the game plan. A shallow fence, for instance, may call for the pitcher to keep his deliveries low in order to induce grounders rather than fly balls that may reach the seats. On the other hand, if the fence is deep, or if there is no fence at all, the pitcher can throw higher pitches to create long fly balls. Interestingly, a larger ball park allows the pitcher and the catcher to explore more weaknesses in the hitters.

The game starts with a plan—a plan that should call for adjustments from inning to inning. It often requires pitch by pitch adjustments as well. The more skilled and versatile the pitcher, the better he will be able to deal with the strategy of the game.

It is important for the catcher to be on the same page with his pitcher. From knowing the goals of the pitcher's daily workouts to clearly understanding his competitive intentions, the catcher should be totally involved.

GATHERING INFORMATION ABOUT HITTERS

Developing a background of facts about opposing hitters may help the pitcher in the game, as well as in practice sessions. Obtaining this information enables the pitcher to plan his attack in advance. A comparison of the pitcher's strengths and weaknesses with the strengths and weaknesses of the batters may supply the necessary criteria for identifying effective strategy. Most importantly, however, the pitcher and the catcher should work together in securing information about the opposing hitters. Together, they should observe the opposing team's batting practice session. On road trips, it is helpful if pitchers and catchers sit in a group and discuss game strategy. For his part, the catcher must always be on the lookout for any tactics that will take advantage of the weaknesses of the opposition or which complement the strengths of his own teammates.

Collecting and filing this information is important. Recalling it is a must. Some catchers have a great memory and a knack for remembering details about every hitter. Some do not. If the catcher is not blessed with a good memory, he should keep a notebook and jot down details on each hitter. Not only should each catcher work to improve his ability to see details, he should also work equally hard on his recall abilities. While improving his skills in these areas, the catcher should become a good note taker.

The catcher can also get a good bead on what types of pitches to use on different batters by observing their stance, stride, swing, and disposition. Other factors, such as natural ability and game situations, can add further to the catcher's collection of information on hitters. If information concerning a particular hitter is limited, however, the general factors described in the following sections on stances, position of hands, warm-up swings, game observations and game performances may help guide the catcher and pitcher until better knowledge becomes available to them.

PROBABLE WEAKNESSES AND STRENGTHS OF VARIOUS STANCES

Open Stance

The hitter with an open stance will probably be strong on inside pitches. Since his hips are already pointing toward the pitch, he will tend to be weaker on outside pitches.

Accordingly, the pitcher, should keep his pitches away from this hitter. He can throw inside to him, as long as those pitches are not in the strike zone. In order to truly cross up this particular batter, and to prevent him from waiting on pitches, the pitcher should never throw all his pitches outside–to the batter's weakness.

Occasionally, hitters adjust. For example, they may change their stride or move closer to the plate. The catcher should always be looking for adjustments like these so that he and the pitcher can counter them. They may even decide to counter by throwing a few pitches to the batter's strength. At the very least, the pitcher should alter his pattern of pitches. To be effective, however, every change of pattern must be evident to the hitter. Once the batter is aware of the change, he will try to adjust to it. It is at that point that the pitcher and catcher can set him up for a pitch he does not expect.

Closed Stance

From a closed stance, the batter will probably hit the ball well into right field, because he usually is effective at hitting the outside pitch. He will hit the ball to left field only if he is strong. Therefore, the pitcher should throw inside to this hitter, so he can jam him with good fastballs on the inside part of the plate. Without the benefit of any previous knowledge of this hitter, the only clue is his stance. A closed stance indicates a possible weakness on inside pitches. Having said all of this about weakness of the closed-stance hitter, it is important to note that the closed stance is also used by many power hitters. These hitters are strong enough to get around on the inside pitch.

Straightaway Stance
The batter with a straightaway stance is capable of hitting to all fields. In high school and college ball, he will probably hit more balls to center and to right than to left field. Accordingly, an attempt should be made to keep the ball low and to favor the inside part of the strike zone until more can be learned about the batter's hitting habits.

POSITION OF HANDS

Besides the stance, there are many other mannerisms and techniques used by the batter that may reveal his weaknesses. While many clues may exist, they are often hard to find. As such, it sometimes takes a very keen eye to discover them. For instance, careful attention to the hitter's method of hitting may provide many tips. The position of the batter's hands, for example, will often expose his strengths and weaknesses. If he holds his hand high, with the bat in a perpendicular position, the batter is indicating that he prefers to hit low pitches. The batter who holds the bat in a horizontal position shows that he favors high pitches.

WARM-UP SWINGS

A batter's warm-up swing often discloses the type of pitch he favors. A level swing may indicate that the batter's best hitting zone is in the area that he is practicing his swings. Practice swings in the high part of the strike zone, on the other hand, show a possible preference for high pitches; while practice swings in the low strike zone may reveal a liking for low pitches. These mannerisms, however, only offer suppositions about the strengths and weaknesses of the hitters. They only offer a starting point for competition. Closer observation during game situations will reveal more pertinent information.

GAME OBSERVATIONS

Observing the batter's swing under game conditions is another method of establishing a meaningful background on the hitter. If the batter has a long sweeping swing, he will probably encounter difficulties with inside pitches. If he has a looping, golf-type swing, he is likely better at hitting low pitches. If the batter pulls his hips away from home plate when he swings, he shows an apparent weakness in hitting outside pitches. If the batter shows over-eagerness by starting his swing too early, he reveals that he is probably vulnerable to off-speed pitches. A particular style or method of swinging the bat may or may not indicate a weakness, however. Therefore, it is the catcher's responsibility to determine whether a weakness indicated actually exists. If one does, he should plan accordingly until other information substantiates or refutes this indication.

GAME PERFORMANCES OF HITTERS

Actual game results provide the most reliable source for gathering data on hitters because it is during the game that all the clues are assembled and measured. Only during the game, for example, does the batter indicate whether he is adept at hitting the curveball or whether he favors a high pitch over a low one. It is also during live action that the hitter shows whether or not he is a first-ball hitter. Furthermore, the game situations will tell the opponent how good a hitter is with men on base.

A catcher should always observe and collect such information on hitters. Many catchers help themselves by keeping a notebook on hitters, while others prefer keeping such information in their heads. Either method is good. The key is that the catcher carefully examine the hitting style of each batter and then plan accordingly.

Details are important. The position of the hitter's hands reveals something about the hitter. The stance also provides valuable information. The swing, too, is also important. Each offers a clue to the pitcher and the catcher on how to pitch to that hitter. Regardless of how much information they have, however, the pitcher and catcher should keep adding information as it becomes available to them.

These simple clues merely offer the first hints about the hitter. These factors should not be relied upon completely, however, because they do not always provide a complete picture. The hitter, for example, may do something entirely out of the ordinary when he strides to hit, such as starting with an open stance, but then striding in such a way that he ends up in a closed stance. All of these clues must be collectively taken into consideration. They must be observed by both the catcher and the pitcher, and their plan of attack should be developed accordingly.

UNORTHODOX BATTERS

An unorthodox method may be quite successful for some hitters. As such, the strengths and weaknesses of these hitters are often difficult to assess. Stan Musial, for example, was one of baseball's greatest hitters, yet his style was very unorthodox. Musial hit from an exaggerated closed stance and positioned himself in the extreme outside back corner of the batter's box. This stance and position suggested two possible weaknesses. Musial was weak on neither.

Some hitters, orthodox and unorthodox, do not have a discernible weakness. After checking their stride, swing, and position at the plate, the catcher concludes that no weakness is evident. The hitter appears to hit low pitches as well as he hits high ones; he hits inside and outside pitches equally well; and he has power to all fields. Obviously, an individual can reach the conclusion that he is a good all-around hitter, one who forces the pitcher to match strength against strength. In this instance, the pitcher must be at his best to win the duel.

STRATEGY BASED ON PITCHER'S ABILITY

The catcher should develop strategy that is essentially based on the pitcher's strengths, although he should also explore the batter's weaknesses. In the end, however, it is best that the pitcher and catcher exploit the pitcher's strengths rather than the batter's weaknesses.

In most cases, when faced with a key situation, the catcher should rely on the pitcher's most effective pitch, even if it means putting the pitcher's strength against the hitter's strength. Any other approach is based on guesswork. The pitcher should realize the gravity of the situation. If he is a fastball pitcher, for example, then he should go with the fastball. After all, it is not only his best pitch, but also the pitch in which he has the most confidence. If it turns out that the pitcher uses is best pitch but fails, he and the catcher can take solace in the fact that they put forth their best effort. If the pitcher and catcher disagree on what type of pitch they should use, the catcher should accede to the pitcher's request. It is always better for the pitcher to use a pitch he feels comfortable with than to throw a pitch he doesn't feel good about, just to satisfy the catcher. If several instances occur in which the two disagree, then they should meet on the mound and discuss the situation. The catcher should explain his reasons for calling certain pitches, and the pitcher should explain his reasons for disagreeing with the catcher. By talking it over, the two should then be able to agree on a plan of operation. The key to calling a good game or making a call the pitcher likes is trust.

PATTERNS OF SIGNAL CALLING

Developing a pattern of signal calling is considered to be unwise, because the opposition can learn the pattern and anticipate the type of pitch that may be thrown. If the batter is uncertain as to the kind of pitch and the speed of the pitch he will see, he will be less likely to time the pitch properly. Accordingly, the pitcher should try to keep the batter off balance and destroy his timing. He should not allow the hitter to develop a routine.

SETTING UP HITTERS

The term "setting up the hitter" is often used when discussing hitting strategy. It simply means that the pitcher and catcher lead the batter to believe that a certain pitch will be thrown, yet surprise him by not throwing the expected pitch. The pitcher who has an outstanding curveball, for example, may "set up a batter" by throwing a curveball for a strike and either a curveball or a fastball for another strike. With two strikes on him, then, the hitter may logically conclude that the pitcher will come with his best pitch, the curveball. In this instance, however, the pitcher may choose to throw a fastball close to, but not in, the strike zone. Throwing the fastball out of the strike zone serves two purposes: (1) it may cause the batter to swing and miss for strike three; or (2) it may create uncertainty, in which case, the batter is set up for the curveball.

A pitcher with poor control should not attempt to set up hitters, because he may not be able to throw to a particular area. Pitchers with overpowering stuff, on the other hand, need not indulge in the practice of trying to deceive the hitter. Even though the batter may know what pitch is coming, he may not be able to get around on the pitch, anyway, because the pitcher is so strong.

KNOWLEDGE OF OFFENSE AND DEFENSE

All aspects of the offense and the defense of both teams must be evaluated by the catcher before he arrives at an effective game plan. The catcher must know the pitcher's best pitches. He should also consider the weaknesses of the opposing hitters, plus their approach, style, and baserunning skills. All of these factors, as well as his own team's defensive skill and strategy, will help the catcher with his decision making.

HABITS OF BASERUNNERS

A sound background of the habits of each baserunner can supply the catcher with important information. Impatience and over-eagerness on the part of a baserunner indicate that the catcher may call for a pitchout and attempt to pick the runner off base. The catcher may also find it a good idea to try to catch the runner off base after a swinging strike, especially since baserunners often indicate their intentions by the way they take their lead off the base.

BATTER'S INTENTIONS

The batter often shows his intentions by the position he takes in the batter's box or by the manner in which he moves. If he intends to bunt, for example, he often drops a big hint by squaring up too early in the pitcher's delivery. On the hit-and-run, he may reveal his intentions by moving his back foot toward third base. Then again, he may simply appear tense. If he does, the catcher may ask the pitcher to change his tempo (i.e., to slow down), so the hitter will become even more nervous. As mentioned earlier, the pitcher controls the tempo of the game, because the action does not start until he delivers a pitch. He relies on the catcher, however, to make the astute observations that will help him stay in control.

GLOSSARY

Arm fake. A simulated throwing motion to one base in an attempt to draw a runner off another base.

Closed stance. A stance in which the batter's front foot is placed toward the inside portion of the batter's box, while his back foot is placed toward the outside portion of the batter's box.

Footwork. The steps taken when moving to catch the ball, clearing away from the batter after the catch, and throwing the ball.

Funneling the ball. The movement used by the catcher to position himself in front of the ball, thus enabling him to draw the ball toward the center of his body.

Head fake. A deliberate look at a runner by the player with the ball, in an attempt to cause that runner to stop or move back to the base, thus permitting the player with the ball to throw to another base.

Hinge mitt. A mitt with special stitching in one or more places that forms a crease in the rolled padding on its face. This stitching creates a break or bend in the pocket of the mitt in the area of the stitching.

Off-speed pitch. Any pitch that is slower than the normal deliveries of the pitcher, such as a change-of-pace pitch or a slow curveball.

Open stance. A stance in which the batter's front foot is placed toward the outside portion of the batter's box, while his back foot is placed toward the inside portion of the batter's box.

Pickoff play. Any throw made by the pitcher or catcher that attempts to catch a runner off base.

Pitchout. A pitch that is purposely thrown outside the strike zone in an effort to throw out a runner whom the catcher believes will attempt to steal a base. It is also a pitch thrown outside the strike zone in an attempt to pick a runner off base. In either case, the baseman involved should know that the pitchout will be thrown, so that he will be able to break early to cover his base.

Rhythm. The continuous movement involved in catching and throwing the ball.

Rotation. The spin on the ball that is created by hitting or throwing the ball.

Setting up hitters. An attempt to lead the batter to believe that the pitcher is establishing a pattern to his pitches by using a pattern and carefully wasting certain pitches, then, at an opportune time, throwing a pitch that the batter does not expect.

Shifting. The movement used by the catcher to position himself in front of the ball, thus enabling him to catch and throw while maintaining proper balance.

Straightaway stance. A stance in which the batter's feet are parallel to home plate.

Throwing grip. The manner in which the fingers are positioned on the ball when throwing.

Warm-up swing. A practice swing taken by a batter prior to swinging at a pitch, or a swing taken while waiting to hit in the on-deck circle.

Bob Bennett is one of the winningest Division 1 baseball coaches of all time. With an overall collegiate mark of 1,190 wins, Bennett ranks 8th on the NCAA all-time victory list and 4th among active coaches in wins.

Since first taking over as Fresno State's head coach more than three decades ago, the Bulldogs have enjoyed constant success on the field of play, winning or sharing 17 league or division titles, advancing to the NCAA playoffs 19 times, and making trips to the College World Series in 1988 and 1991. His teams have averaged nearly 40 wins per season and are consistently ranked in the National Top 25 polls. Bennett himself has earned league College Coach of the Year honors 13 times, in addition to being named 1988 NCAA Coach of the Year by *The Sporting News*.

Bennett, who is a member of the Fresno State Baseball Hall of Fame as well as a member of the ABCA Hall of Fame, has also been heavily involved in baseball at the international level, serving as a head coach of the U.S. National Team in 1983 and 1986 and serving on the National Team's coaching staff in 1977 and 1979.

Considered by many to be one of the top pitching coaches in the country, Bennett has seen nearly 200 of his players signed to professional contracts. In the process, Bennett has produced 27 All Americans of which eleven were pitchers. Seven of his players have been first round draft picks.

Bennett served as President of the American Baseball Coaches Association in 1987. In January, 2000 he received the Lefty Gomez Award for lifetime contributions to amateur baseball. He is a sought-after clinician and has published over 40 articles in professional coaching magazines over the past 30 years. He is the author of several books including *101 Pitching Drills* and *Pitching from the Ground Up* and has produced several best-selling videotapes. Bob Bennett and his wife, Karen, have three children, Karen, Brad and Todd, and eight grandchildren.

6 ADDITIONAL GREAT BOOKS BY BOB BENNETT

Pitching from the Ground Up
223 pp • $20.00
1-58518-180-3 • 1997

101 Pitching Drills
136 pp • $16.95
1-58518-224-9 • 1999

including four books of Poetry

Words and Rhythms of Baseball
140 pp • $12.95
1-58518-225-7 • 1996

Roots and Wings
132 pp • $12.95
1-58518-226-5 • 1996

A Passion for the Game
148 pp • $14.95
1-58518-150-1 • 2000

Rhymes and Reasons
132 pp • $14.95
1-58518-151-X • 2000

6 EXCEPTIONAL INSTRUCTIONAL VIDEOS BY BOB BENNETT

Pitching from the Ground Up
58 min • $40.00
1-57167-146-3 • 1999

Pitching Drills
57 min • $40.00
1-57167-148-X • 1999

Hitting Fundamentals and Techniques
44 min • $40.00
1-57167-334-2 • 1999

Catching Fundamentals and Techniques
60 min • $40.00
1-57167-147-1 • 1999

Outfield Play Fundamentals and Techniques
50 min • $40.00
1-57167-336-9 • 1999

Baserunning Fundamentals and Techniques
50 min • $40.00
1-57167-335-0 • 1999